Shredding Guitar Workout

Heavy Metal Meets the Thinking Shredder's Technical Practice

German Schauss

Alfred Music
P.O. Box 10003
Van Nuys, CA 91410-0003
alfred.com

Copyright © MMXIV by Alfred Music
All rights reserved. Printed in USA.

No part of this book shall be reproduced, arranged, adapted, recorded, publicly performed, stored in a retrieval system, or transmitted by any means without written permission from the publisher. In order to comply with copyright laws, please apply for such written permission and/or license by contacting the publisher at alfred.com/permissions.

ISBN-10: 1-4706-1518-5 (Book & DVD)
ISBN-13: 978-1-4706-1518-5 (Book & DVD)

Cover Photos
Main photo: Larry Lytle • Baroque ornament: © iStockphoto / Scott Krycia • Back Cover: Crissy Almeida

 Alfred Cares. Contents printed on environmentally responsible paper.

CONTENTS

About the Author 3
    Acknowledgments 3

Introduction 4

Alternate-Picking Workout 5
    Warm-Ups 5
    Chromatic Melodic Patterns 7
    Two-String Pentatonic Shapes 10
    Five Positions of the A Minor Pentatonic Scale ...12
    Pentatonic Melodic Patterns.......................13
    Pentatonic Patterns Using Intervals 16
    Two-String 7th Arpeggios 17
    Three-Octave Two-Note-per-String Arpeggios ... 19
    Arpeggiated Melodic Patterns.....................22
    Single-String Shapes of the Major Scale 25
    Hexatonic Two-String Shapes 27
    Three-Note-per-String Scales 31
    Major Scale Melodic Patterns.....................32
    Major Scale Patterns Using Intervals 35
    Major Scale Patterns Using Arpeggios 46
    Three-Note-per-String Fingerings
        for the Seven-String Guitar 50
    Speed Development 51
        Rhythm Pyramid 55

Sweep Picking 56
    Two-String Sweeping...................................58
    Three-String Sweeping................................66
    Five-String Sweeping...................................69
    Arpeggio Shapes for the Seven-String Guitar.....75

Legato Technique 77
    Legato Warm-Ups..77
    One- and Two-String Legato Patterns 79
    Legato Phrases Across the Fretboard..........82

Tapping 86
    Tapping Scales and Arpeggios 89
    Tapping Triad Arpeggios 92
    Tapping 7th Arpeggios................................94

Conclusion 96

A Note About the Video

The DVD video corresponds to lessons in the book and the two are intended to be used together. The DVD contains MP3s to make it more fun and easier to learn. To access the MP3s, go to the DVD menu and select DVD-ROM, where you will find audio tracks that correspond with specific lessons.

There is a video lesson for every example marked with this icon: ▶. Every example is numbered, whether it is demonstrated on the video or not. Some examples are subdivided and labeled with letters. The letters that are demonstrated on the video are circled.

Have fun!

ABOUT THE AUTHOR

German Schauss is a guitarist, composer, author, and educator who teaches at Berklee College of Music and other international music schools. He performs and tours as the leader of his own band and with other internationally known artists. German writes music for commercials, TV, and video games, and has been named one of the 50 fastest guitarists of all time by *Guitar World* magazine. The author of *Shredding Bach* (#34922), *Shredding Paganini* (#37468), *Shredding the Composers* (#39378), and *The Total Shred Guitarist* (#36573), German also writes the popular monthly column "Instant Shredding" for Germany's biggest guitar magazine, *Gitarre & Bass*.

German uses and proudly endorses: Schecter Guitars, Bogner Amps, Kemper Amps, Rocktron, PreSonus, Native Instruments, Maxon, Morley, Dunlop, Voodoo Labs, Pigtronix Pedals, DiMarzio, Zoom, Tremol-No, D'Addario Strings, Planet Waves, MakeMusic, and Pedaltrain products.

For more about German Schauss and his music, please visit: www.germanschauss.com

PHOTO BY JI YEON SONG

Acknowledgments

Thank you to my family, friends, and fans around the world for their support, positive thoughts, and love—you are all an inspiration to me! Additionally, thanks to Nat Gunod, Link Harnsberger, and the entire team at Alfred Music.

INTRODUCTION

Welcome to *Shredding Guitar Workout*. This book and DVD package contains an organized collection of exercises to help intermediate and advanced guitar players improve their technique and skills. Beginning players can also learn a lot from these lessons, even if they can't yet play all the exercises.

Remember to practice slowly at first, and make sure you fully understand the concepts in order to gain optimal results. Always practice with your hands *and* head!

There is a lot of information in this book, and it will be wise to structure your practice time. Time is always a limiting factor, so it is important to choose a few exercises from each of the four categories in this book (Alternate-Picking, Sweep Picking, Legato Technique, and Tapping) and practice them in a different key every day. Keep rotating the exercises, so that, eventually, you will have practiced them all without neglecting a single category. Building up good technique and practice habits will take time and a lot of work, but when you set goals, organize your schedule, and have a clear direction, you can achieve anything!

Keep on shredding!

ALTERNATE-PICKING WORKOUT

Warm-Ups

Warming up and getting your hands synchronized is extremely important and will take a lot of practice and patience. The examples below illustrate simple *chromatic* (half step) runs across all six strings, first with a triplet feel and then with a sixteenth-note feel. Practice these exercises with a metronome and begin slowly. Using *alternate picking*, alternating up and down picking strokes continuously.

Ex. 1

Continue to the 12th fret and then play in reverse (3–2–1) back to the 1st fret.

After each run through these exercises, increase the tempo on your metronome by 8 to 10 beats per minute. Keep a journal, or log of your tempos, so that there is a record of your progress.

Ex. 2

Continue to the 12th fret and then play in reverse (4–3–2–1) back to the 1st fret.

Shredding Guitar Workout

The following examples are variations of the previous ideas and incorporate *string skipping*, where you jump over one or more strings when playing consecutive notes. Pay extra attention to your picking accuracy and avoid any unnecessary string ringing.

This exercise has a triplet feel.

This next one has a sixteenth-note feel.

Chromatic Melodic Patterns

The following exercises are chromatic patterns, or sequences, in three- and four-note groupings. A pattern or sequence is a repetitive melodic passage that is restated at higher or lower pitches. These examples, which consist of different combinations of ascending and descending patterns, will improve your left/right-hand coordination and will facilitate good technique. Practice all examples slowly, and once you have full control over the patterns, transfer them to the other string sets. Always use a metronome to keep track of your speed and progress.

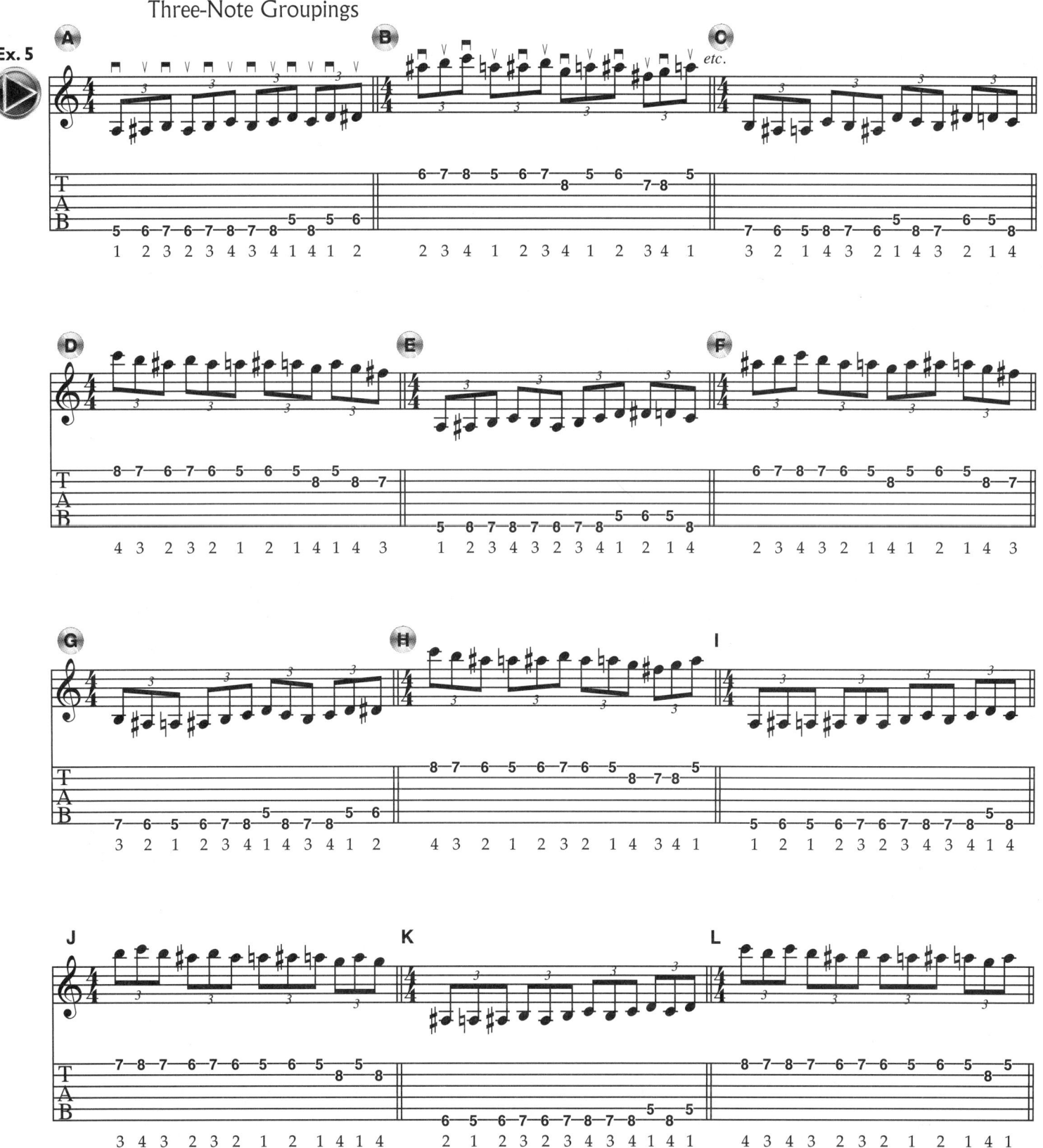

Ex. 6 — Four-Note Groupings

SHREDDING GUITAR WORKOUT

Chromatic Patterns Using Intervals

Ex. 7

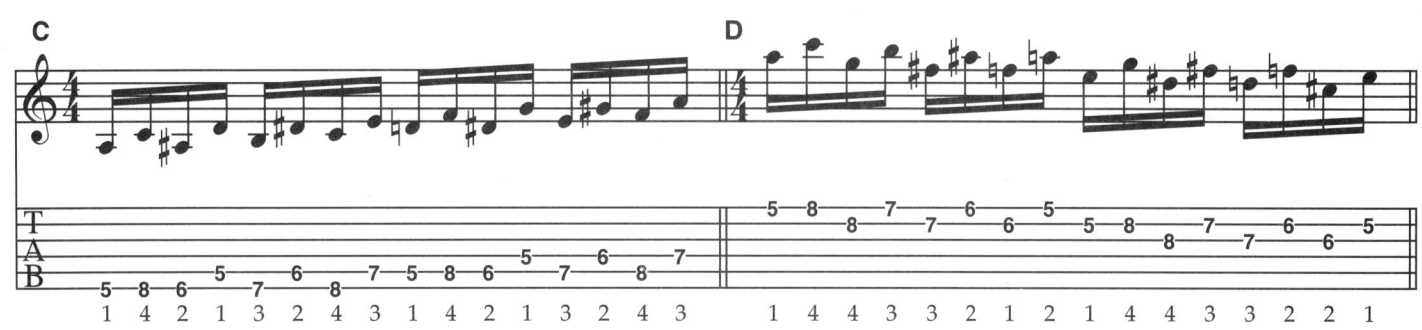

Two-String Pentatonic Shapes

Alternate picking with two-note-per-string patterns can be challenging, since it requires fast movement from string to string. One of the most basic (yet also one of the most important) scales is the *minor pentatonic scale*. The notes of the A Minor Pentatonic scale are: A–C–D–E–G. The formula in terms of scale steps is: 1–♭3–4–5–♭7. This scale, which can be used in many different musical styles and harmonic situations, can be broken down into five basic shapes. Below, you will see diagrams showing these five basic shapes on two strings. The examples following the diagrams illustrate some of the basic patterns that can be applied to these two-string shapes. Move these ideas to the other string sets as well.

Form 1

Form 2

Form 3

Form 4

Form 5

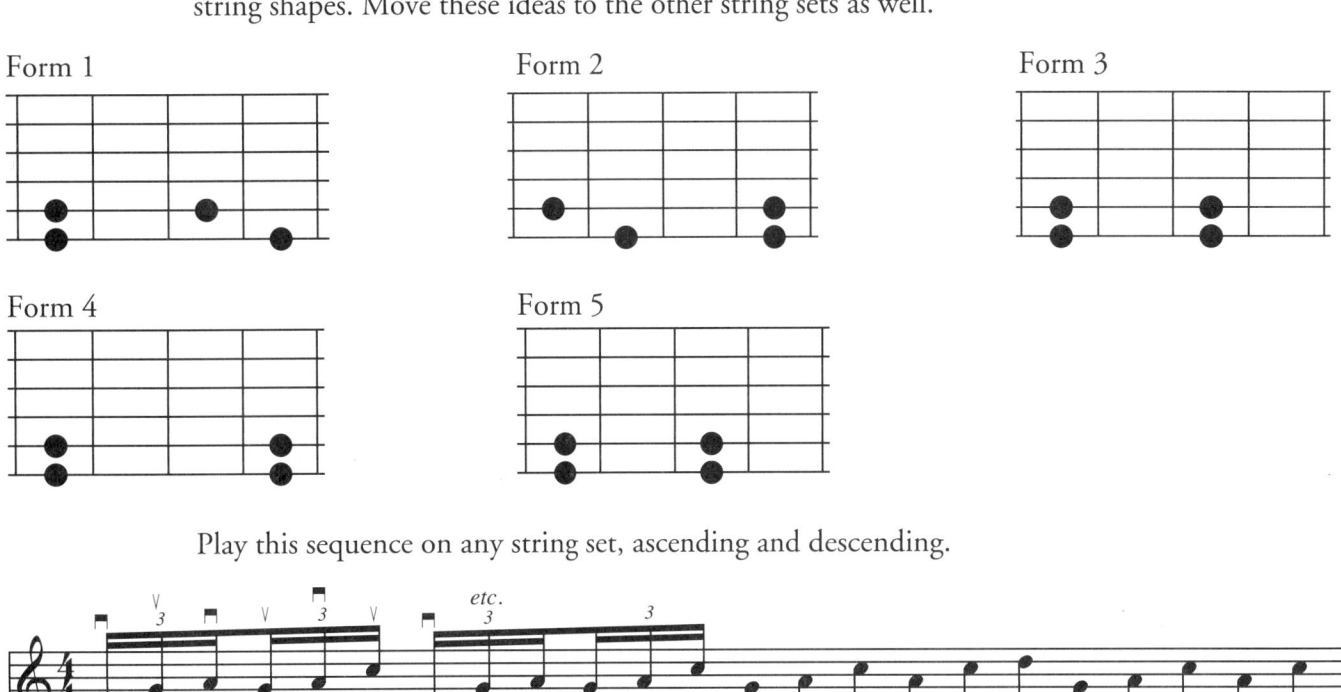

Play this sequence on any string set, ascending and descending.

Ex. 8

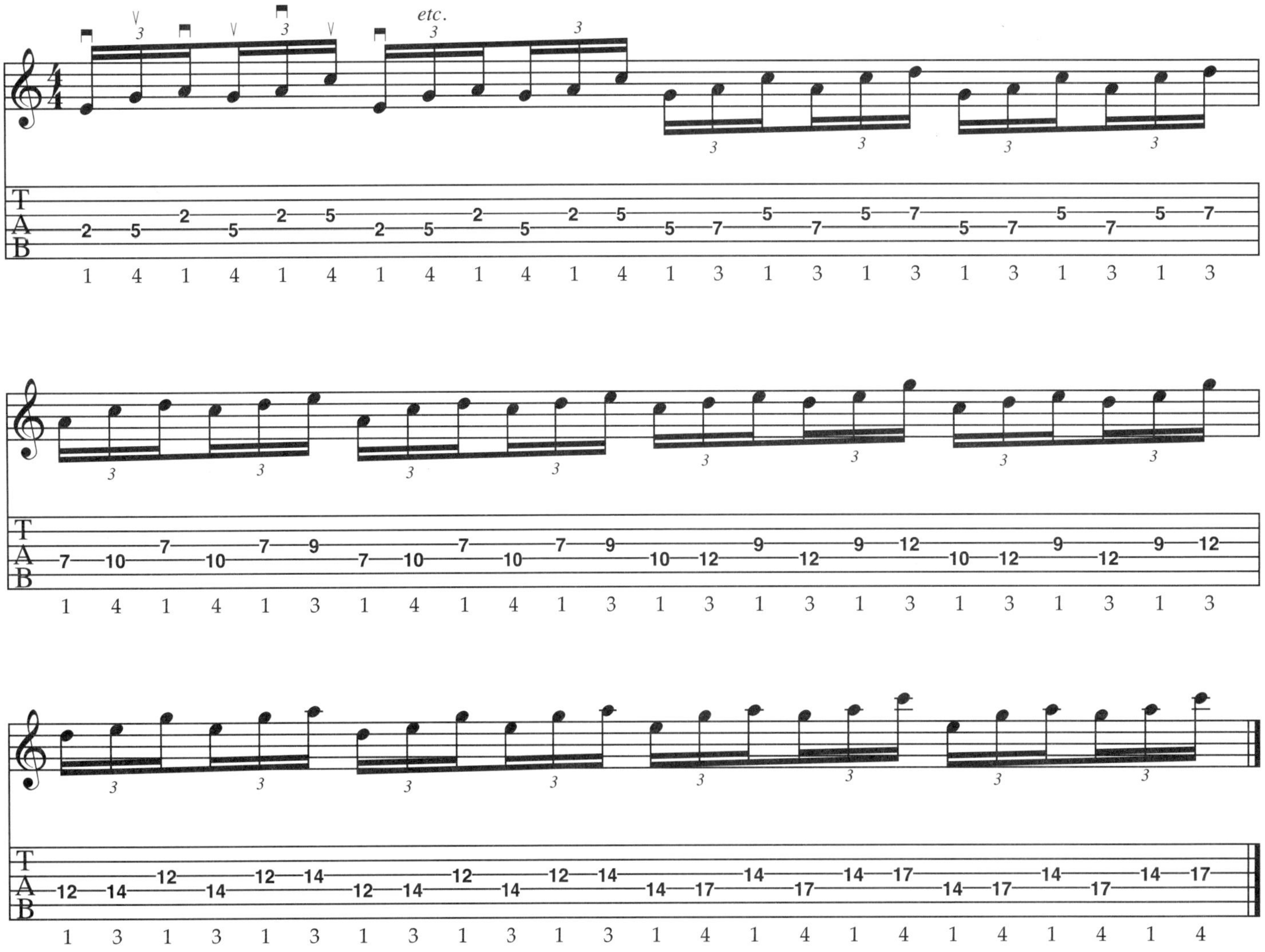

Play all five shapes in ascending and descending patterns. Move the shapes to higher and lower octaves as well.

Ex. 9

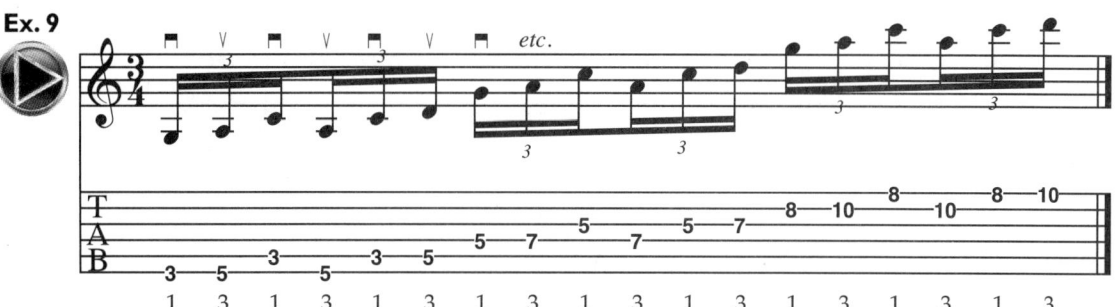

Play the following string-skipping sequence, both ascending and descending.

Ex. 10

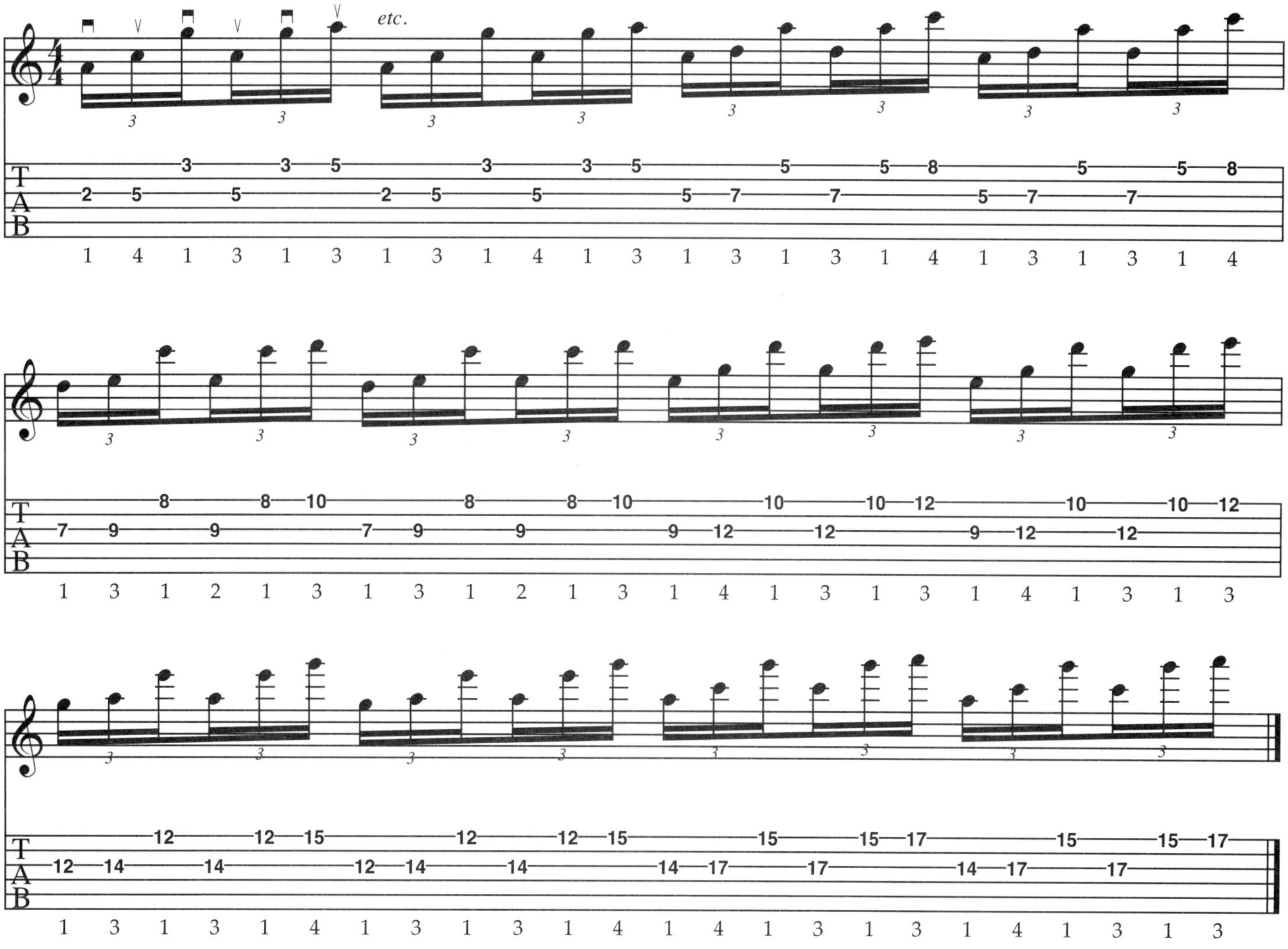

Five Positions of the A Minor Pentatonic Scale

The diagrams below show the five shapes, or positions, of the A Minor Pentatonic scale. The most common shape is the one that starts from the root. It is essential, however, to learn all the shapes in order to develop a solid understanding of the scale and fretboard. This will enable you to play fluently in different positions and utilize the full range of the guitar.

Starting from the ♭7th

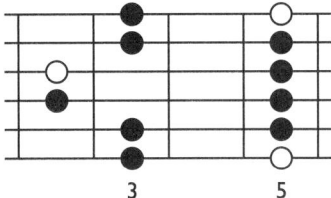

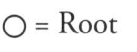
○ = Root

Starting from the root

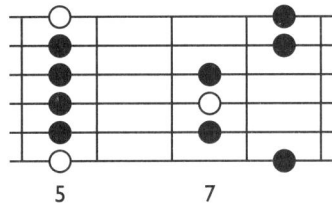

Starting from the ♭3rd

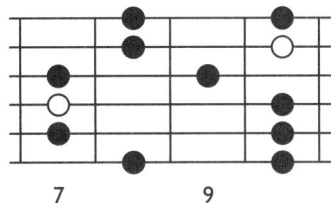

Starting from the 4th

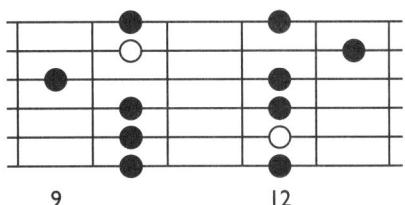

Starting from the 5th

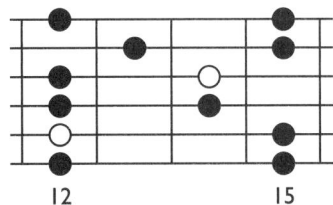

Pentatonic Melodic Patterns

Now that you are familiar with the different pentatonic positions, let's take a look at some melodic patterns. These sequences are all played using the root-position shape and are in three-, four-, five-, and six-note groupings.

Play these exercises in all possible positions and string sets, and use a metronome to measure and track your speed.

Three-Note Groupings

Shredding Guitar Workout

Four-Note Groupings

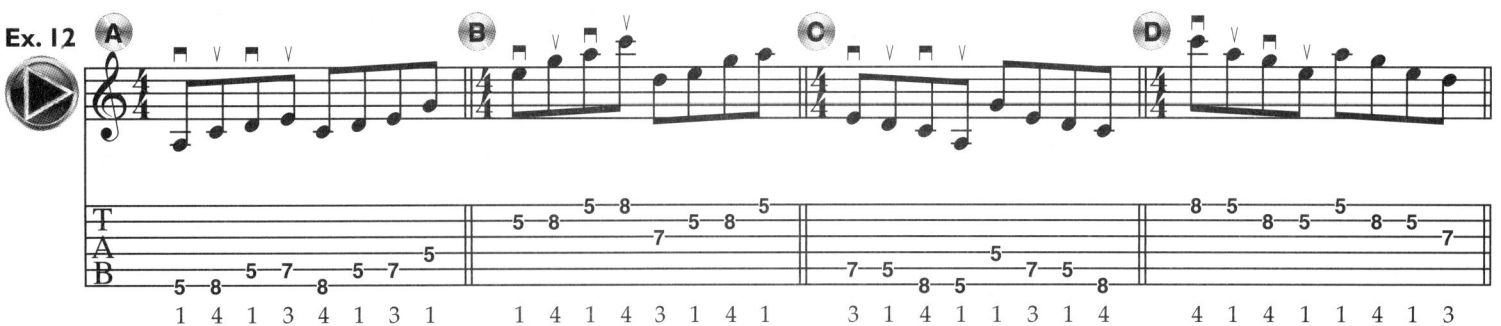

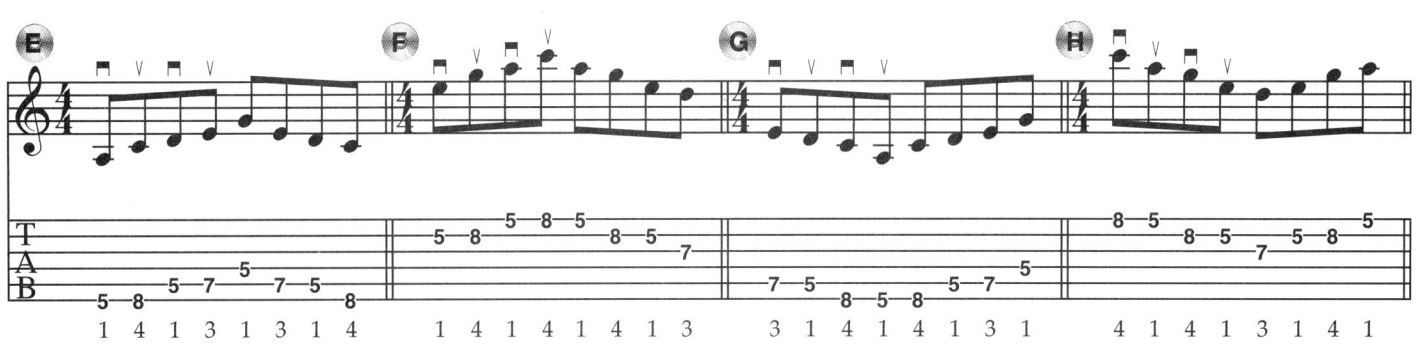

Five-Note Groupings

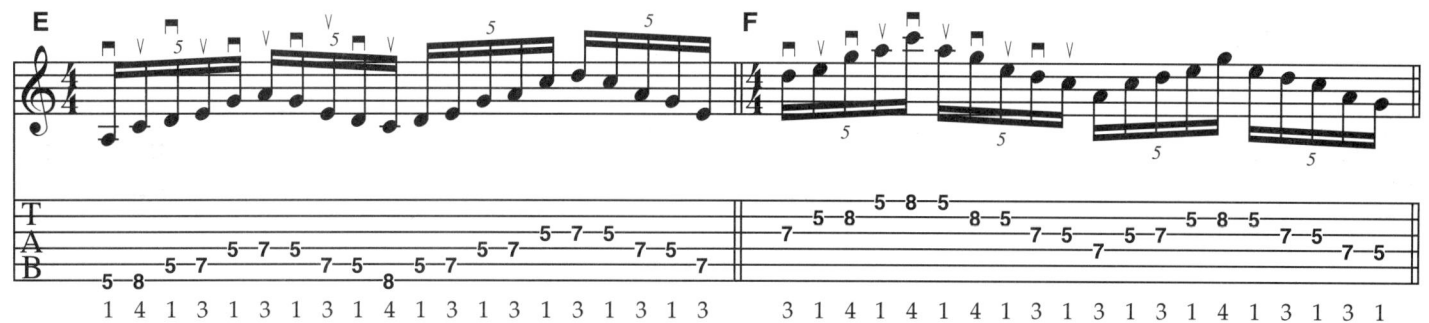

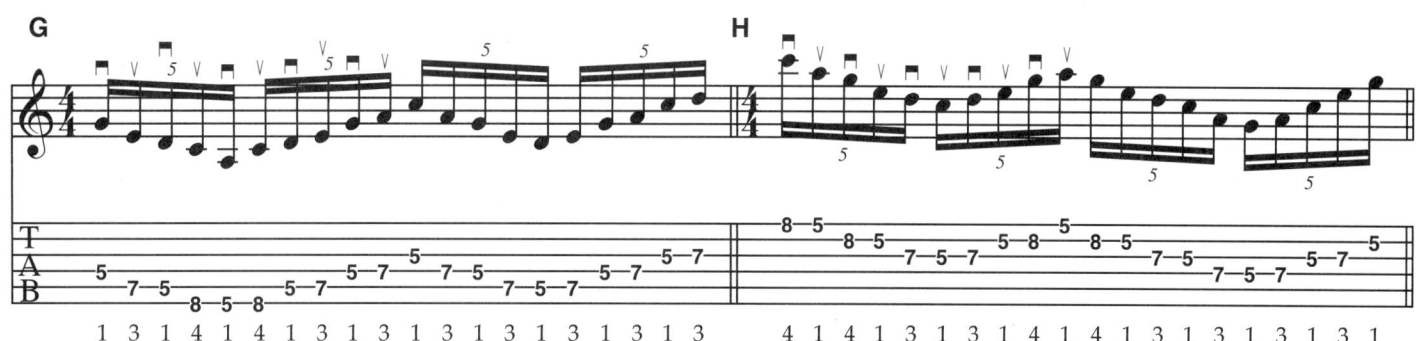

Six-Note Groupings

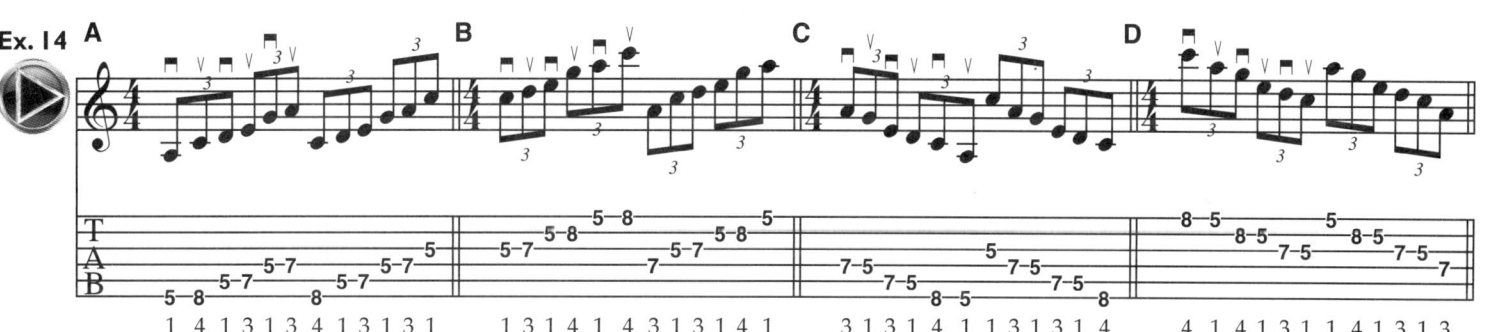

Shredding Guitar Workout

Pentatonic Patterns Using Intervals

Scales can also be played using interval-based sequences. The following examples are patterns based on 4ths and 5ths. Of course, there are many more possibilities, and we encourage you to find and practice them. Begin by practicing these examples slowly, while striving for accuracy and fluency.

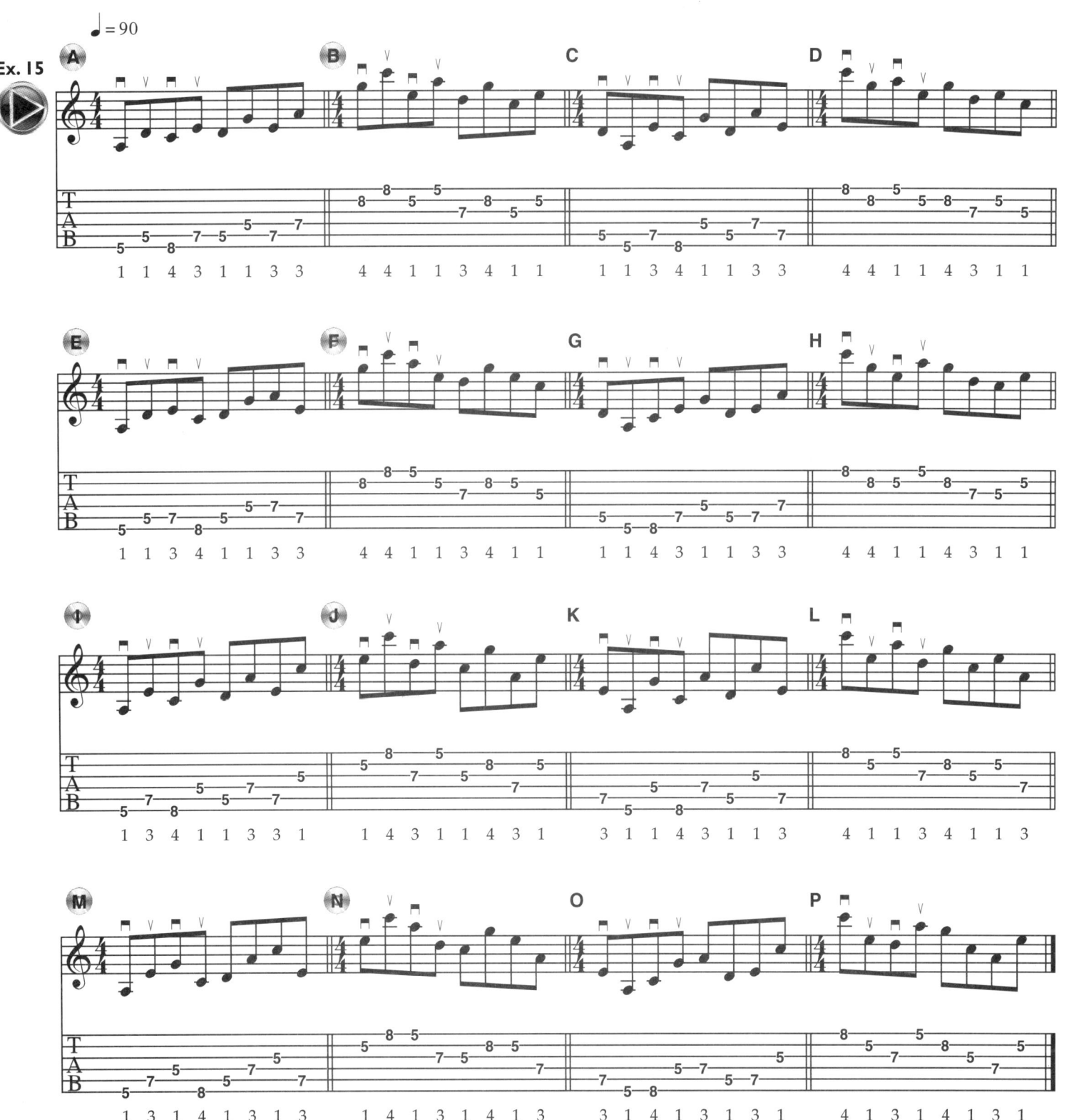

Two-String 7th Arpeggios

Arpeggios are the notes of a chord played consecutively rather than simultaneously (as with a chord). Two-note-per-string arpeggios offer a different approach to playing chord progressions. Below are diagrams for four types of 7th-chord arpeggios: major 7th (Maj7), dominant 7th (7), minor 7th (min7), and minor 7th ♭5 (min7♭5). These shapes are in *3rd inversion*, meaning the bottom note, or first note played, is the 7th of the chord.

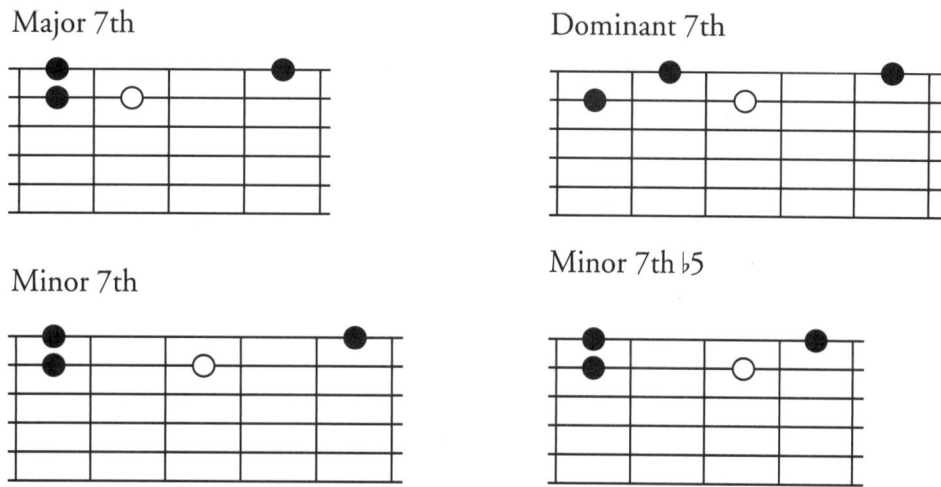

Learn and memorize the shapes above, and then move them to their respective root notes to harmonize a major scale, like C Major:

CMaj7–Dmin7–Emin7–FMaj7–G7–Amin7–Bmin7♭5

The following shapes show the CMaj7 two-string arpeggio in root position and all of its inversions. Learn these different forms and use them as a reference to work out the shapes for the dominant 7th, minor 7th, and minor 7th ♭5 arpeggios.

CMaj7 Shapes

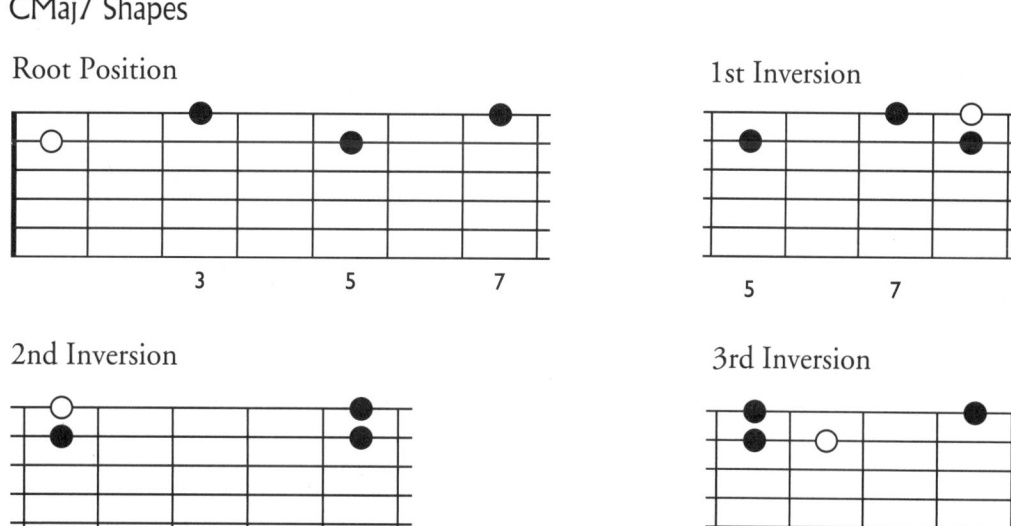

Now that we have established a variety of two-string arpeggio shapes, let's look at some basic patterns. The examples below illustrate ascending and descending patterns in three- and four-note groupings.

— = Position shift.

Basic Two-String Arpeggio Patterns

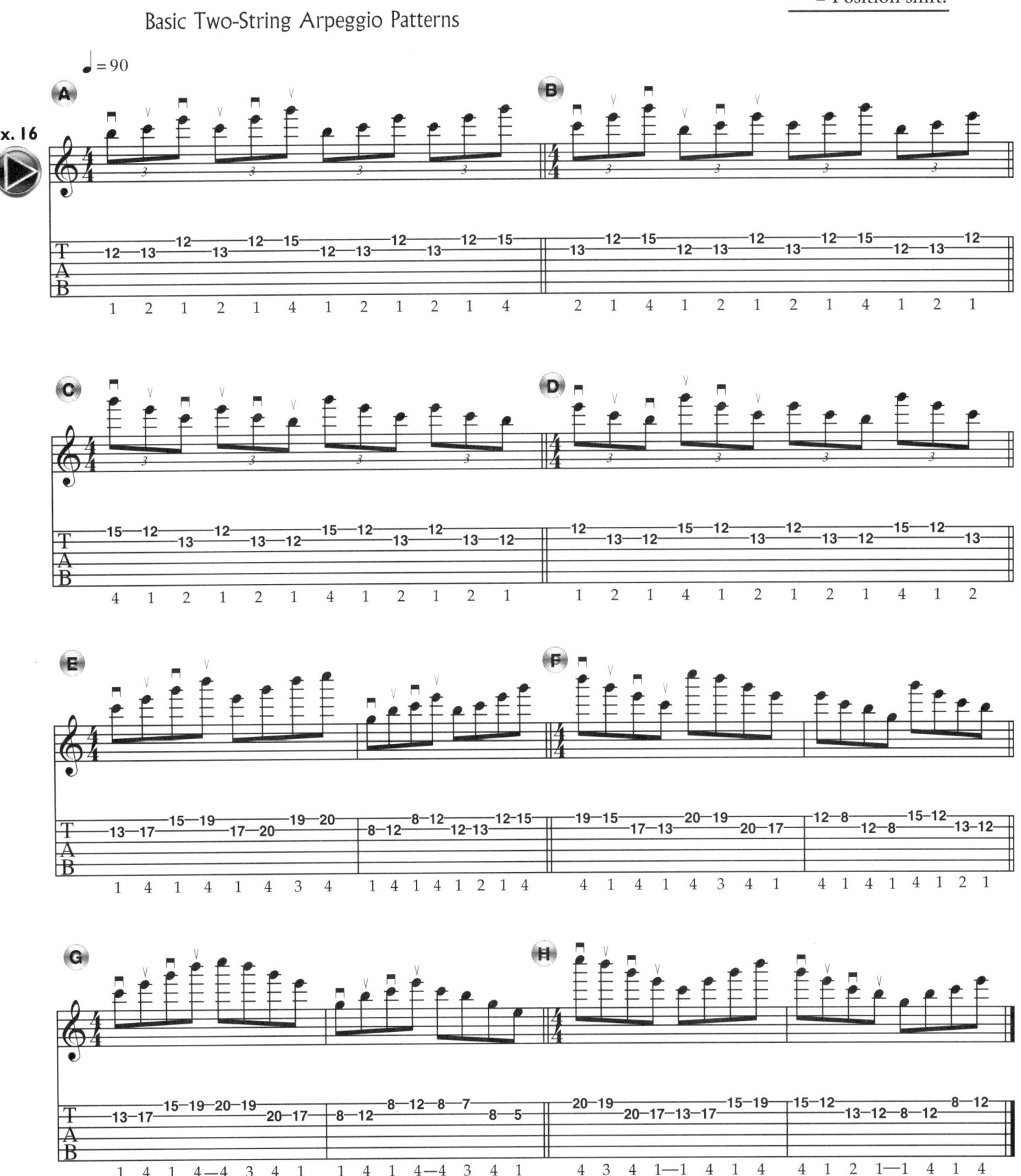

Three-Octave Two-Note-per-String Arpeggios

Once you know all the basic two-string arpeggio shapes, you can move them from string pair to string pair and octave to octave. Below are three-octave shapes for the major 7th, dominant 7th, minor 7th, and minor 7th♭5 arpeggios. Learn and memorize all of these shapes, apply them to different chords and keys, and even try to arpeggiate a simple chord progression.

CMaj7 (2nd Inversion)

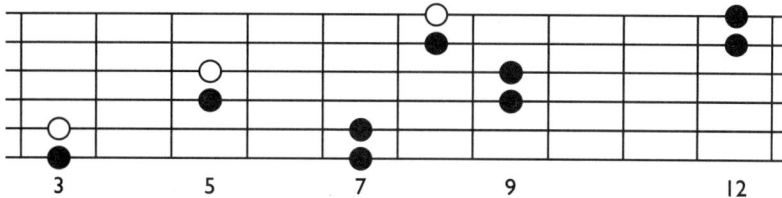

CMaj7 (3rd Inversion)

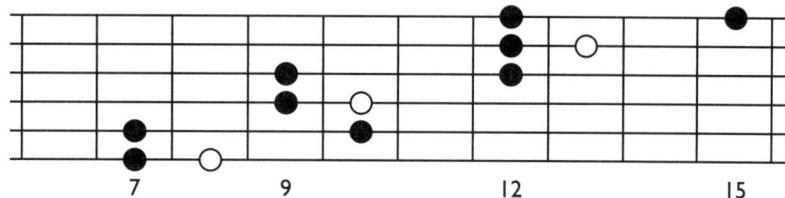

CMaj7 (Root Position)

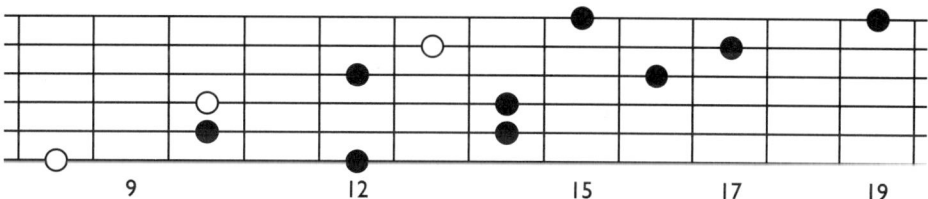

CMaj7 (1st inversion)

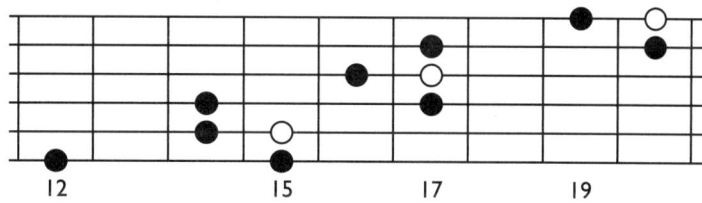

C7 (2nd Inversion)

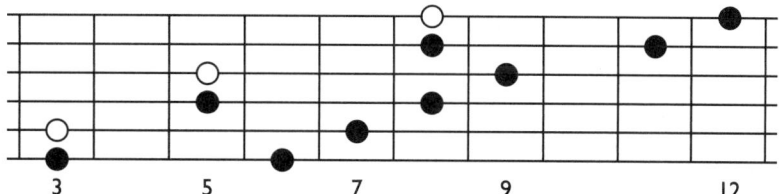

C7 (3rd Inversion)

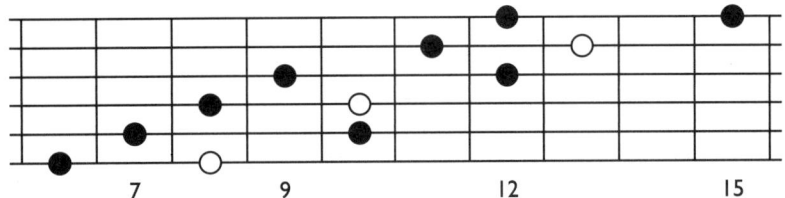

C7 (Root Position)

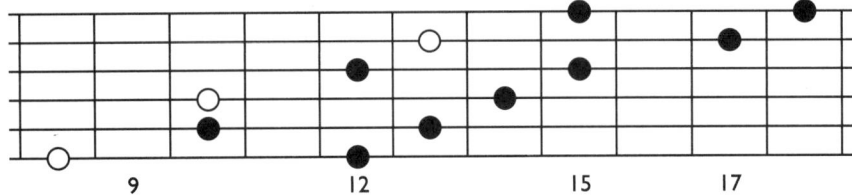

C7 (1st Inversion)

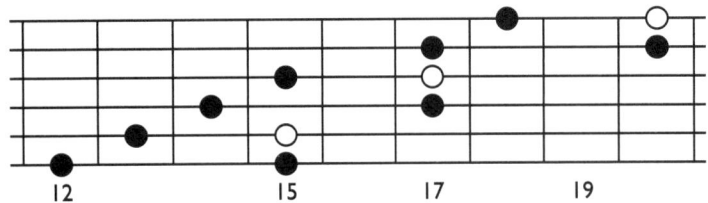

Cmin7 (2nd Inversion)

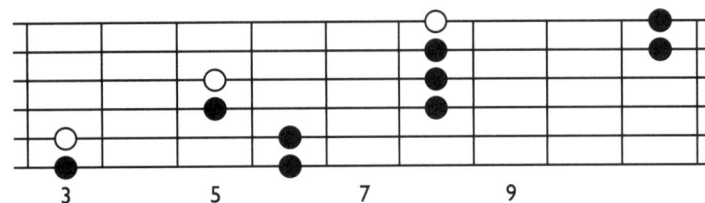

Cmin7 (3rd Inversion)

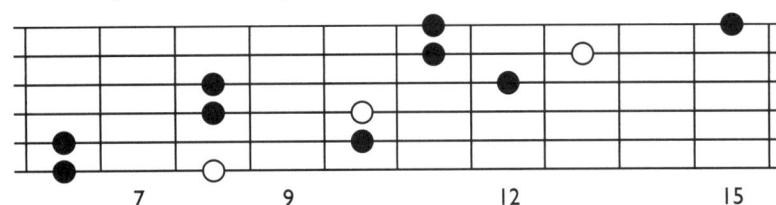

Cmin7 (Root Position)

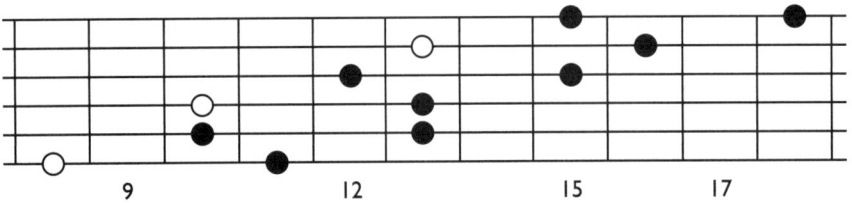

Cmin7 (1st Inversion)

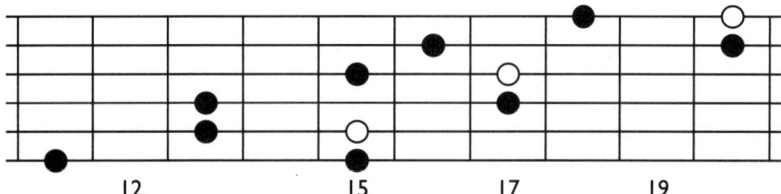

Cmin7♭5 (2nd Inversion)

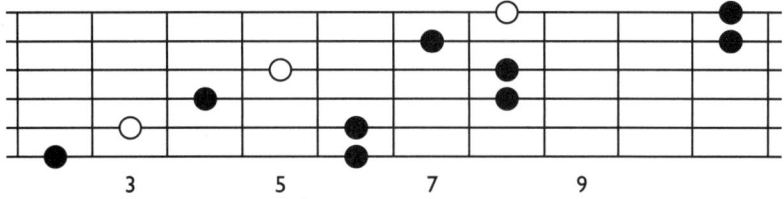

Cmin7♭5 (3rd Inversion)

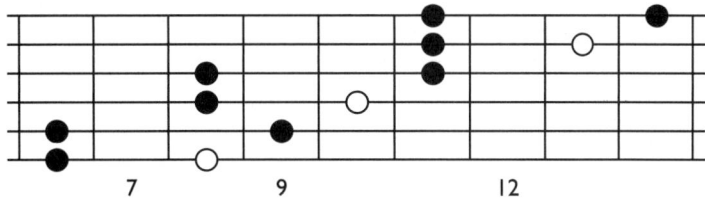

Cmin7♭5 (Root Position)

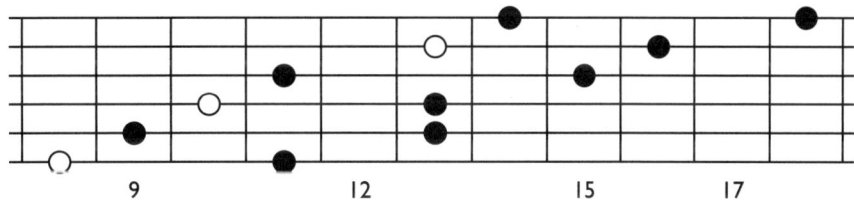

Cmin7♭5 (1st Inversion)

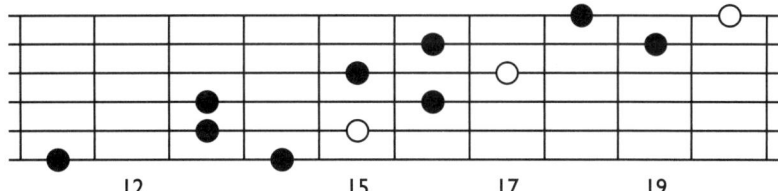

Arpeggiated Melodic Patterns

Following are patterns for the three-octave two-note-per-string arpeggios covered in the previous section. The examples are in three- and four-note groupings, for which you are to use strict alternate picking. Practice carefully and pay close attention to your fingering when shifting positions.

Three-Note Groupings

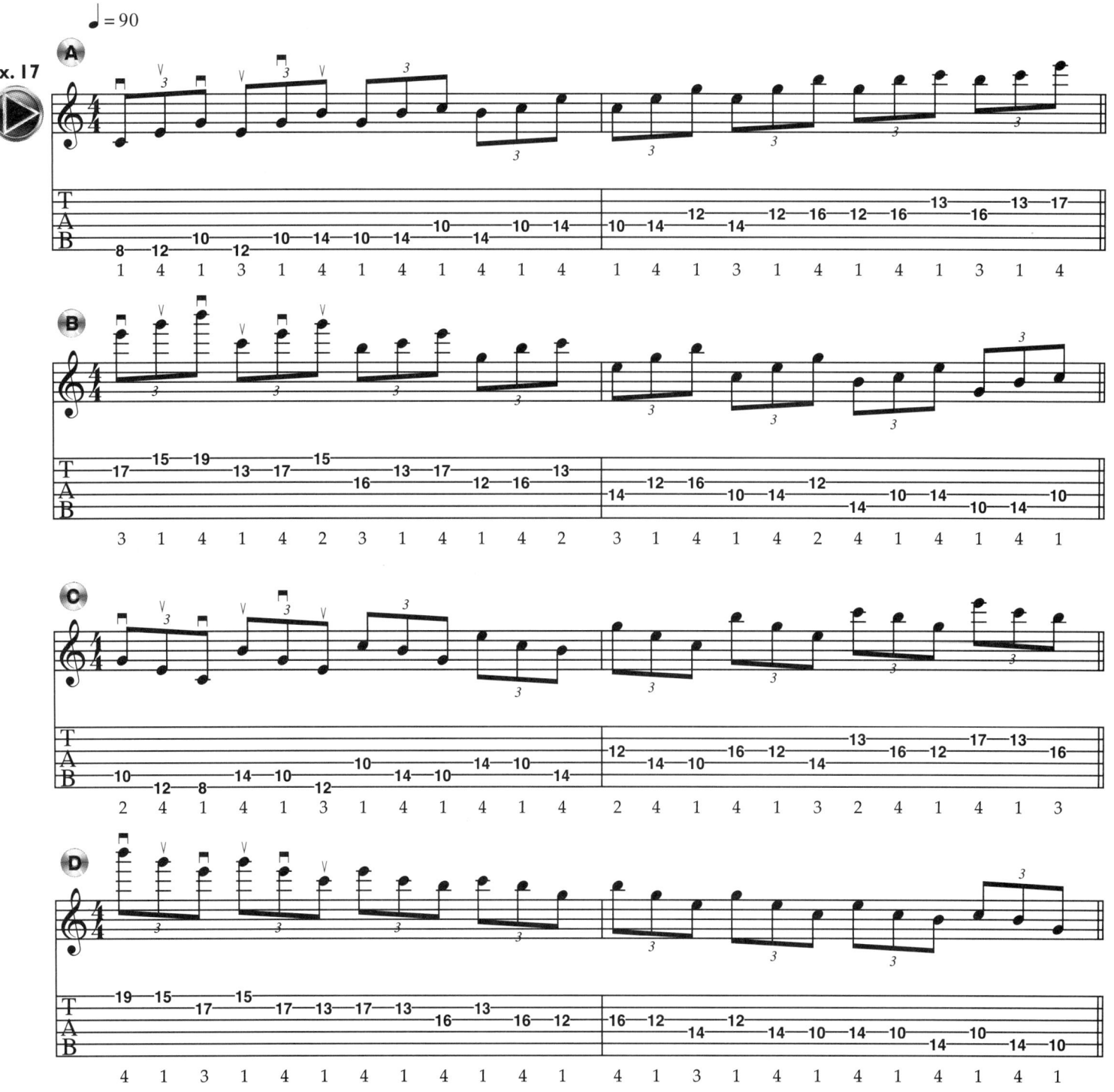

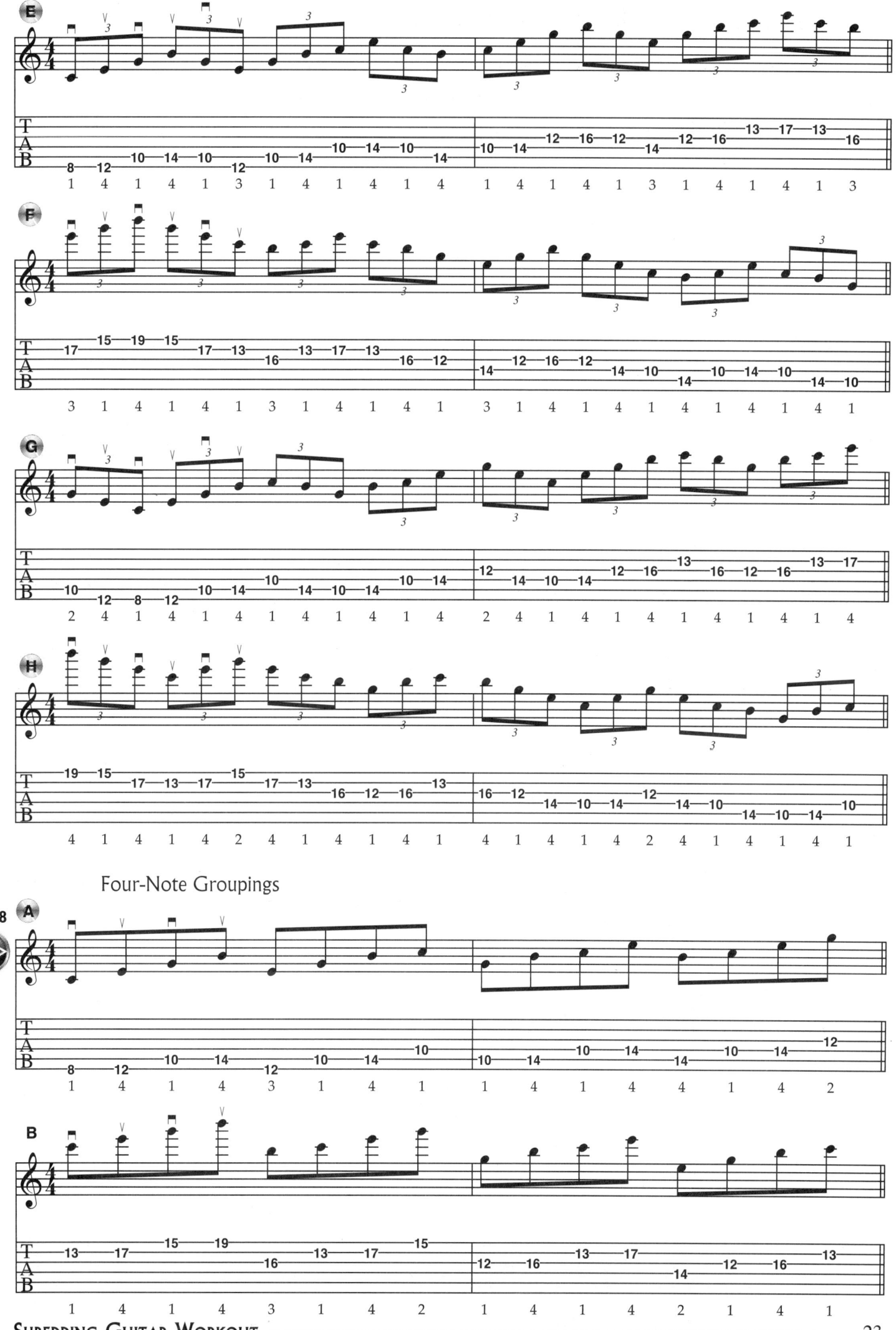

Four-Note Groupings

Shredding Guitar Workout

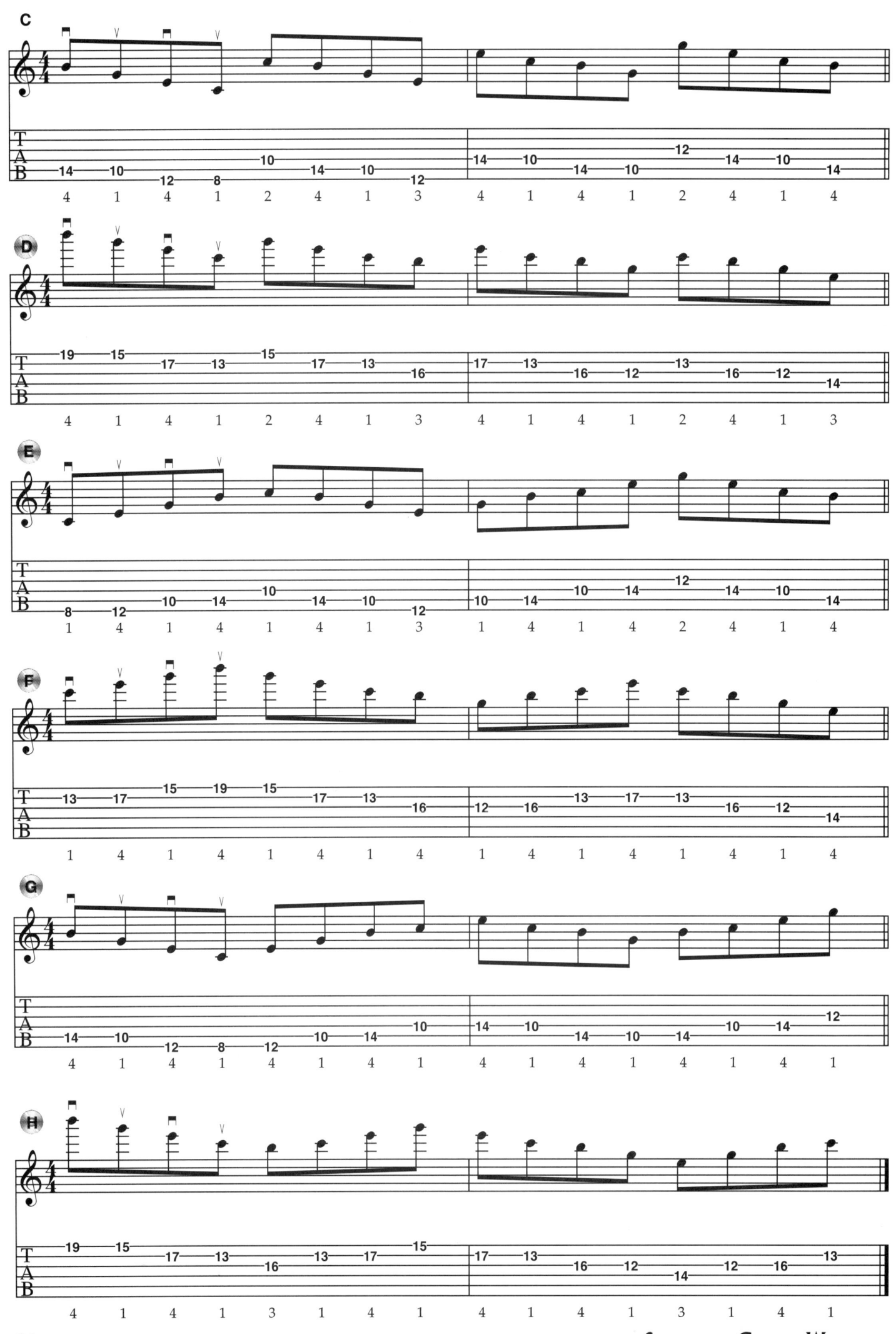

Single-String Shapes of the Major Scale

The *major scale* is one of the most important building blocks in Western music. It consists of seven notes, or *scale degrees* (1–2–3–4–5–6–7), in a particular order of whole steps (two frets) and half steps (one fret) known as the major scale formula. This major scale formula is: whole–whole–half–whole–whole–whole–half. The notes of a C Major scale are: C–D–E–F–G–A–B. To build a different major scale, you just need to start on a different root note and follow the major scale formula.

Below is the C Major scale. Use the major scale formula to derive and practice the other 11 major scales.

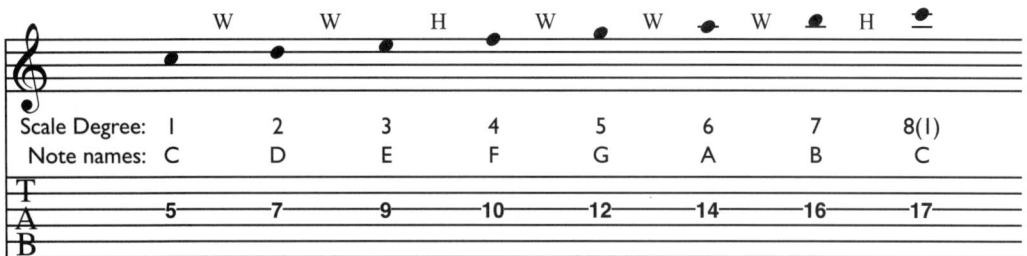

W = Whole step
H = Half step

A scale can be broken down into individual shapes on the guitar. The basic shapes for three-note-per string scales on one string are as follows:

Pattern 1 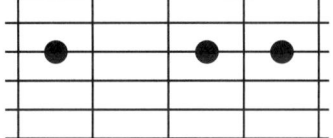 Pattern 2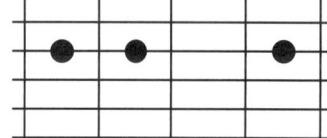

Pattern 3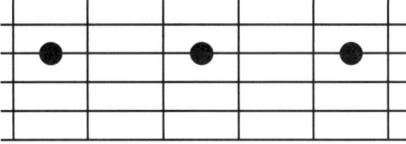

Take the shapes above and align them on all strings, creating a scale like C Major. Use these shapes to practice the single-string patterns.

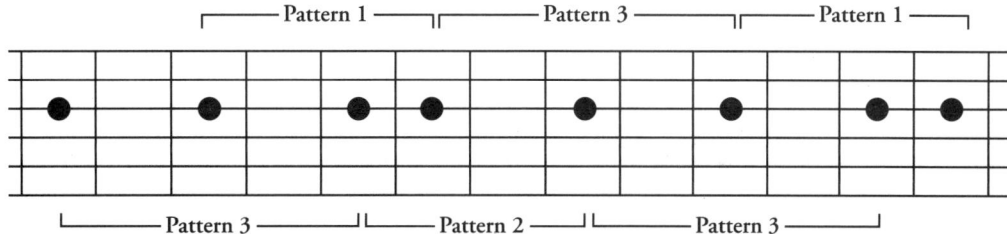

SHREDDING GUITAR WORKOUT

Practice the single-string patterns carefully and pay close attention to your left- and right-hand synchronization. Of course, use a metronome once you understand the pattern and can execute it correctly. The following examples use strict alternate picking and are in the key of G Major/E Minor.

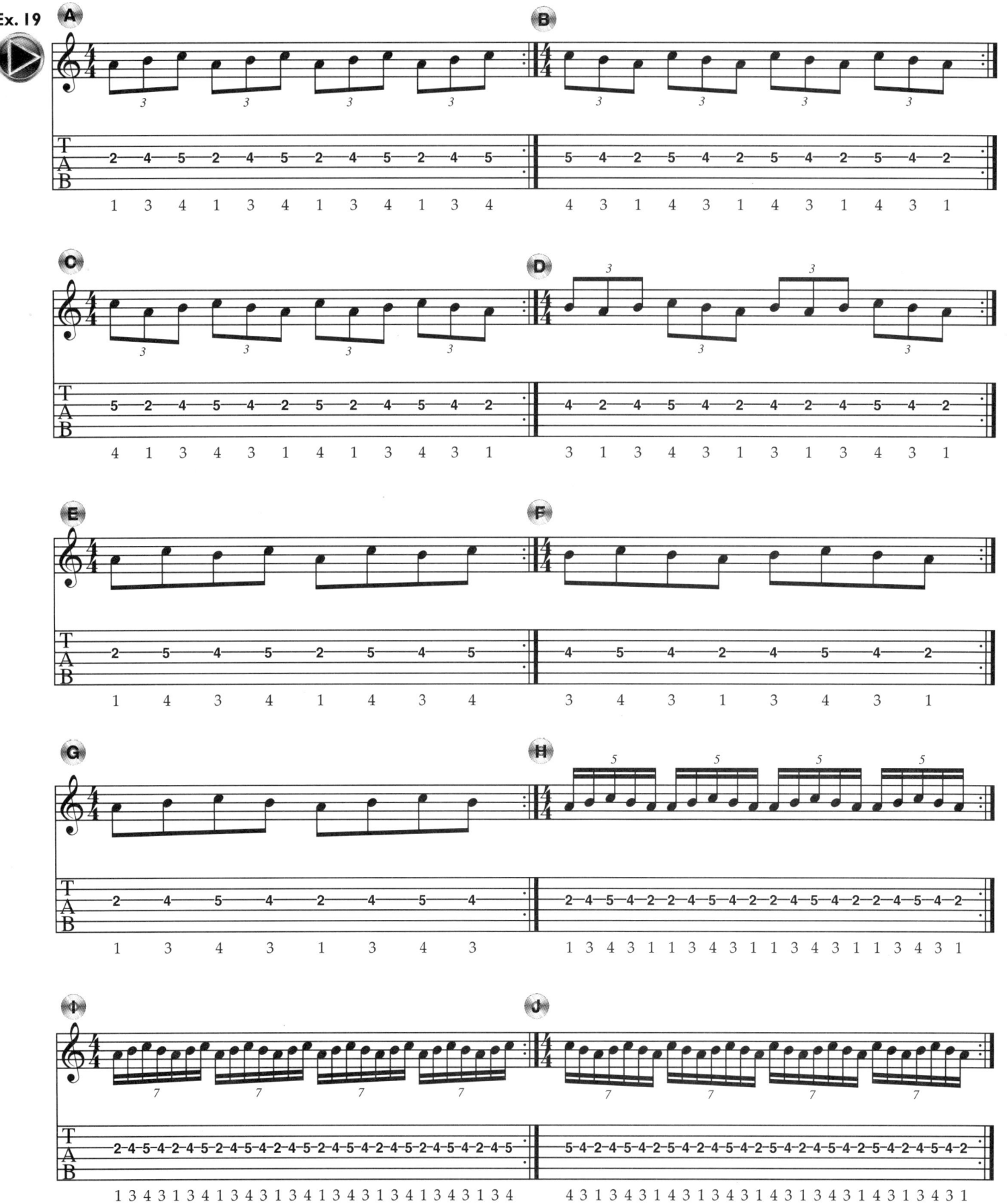

Hexatonic Two-String Shapes

The three-note-per-string scale can also be broken down into two-string shapes and patterns. These seven different shapes, also called *hexatonic scales* (because they consist of six notes each), are the basic building blocks of the scale and can be moved in octaves or aligned across the fretboard to create complete three-note-per-string scales (see page 31 for scale diagrams).

Study the following two-string patterns and move them around the fretboard either chromatically or diatonically and on all string sets. Keep in mind that when you play these patterns on the 2nd and 3rd strings, you will need to adjust the pattern one half step higher on the 2nd string to account for the tuning difference.

Pattern 1
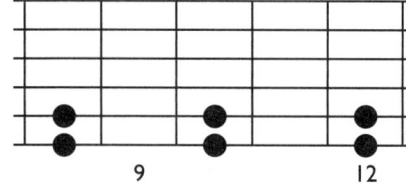

Pattern 2
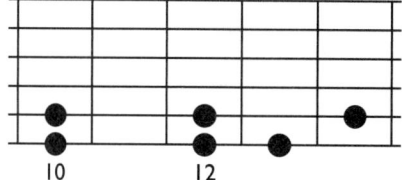

Pattern 3
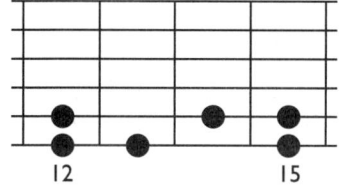

Pattern 4
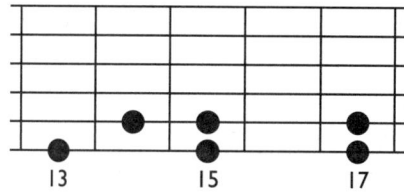

Pattern 5
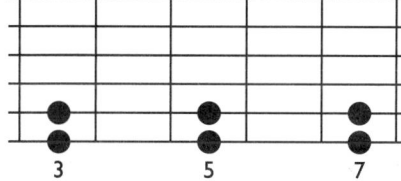

Pattern 6
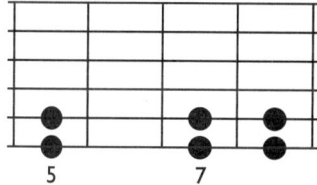

Pattern 7
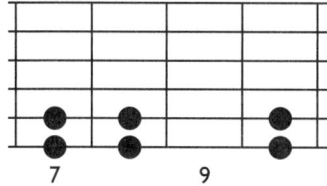

The examples starting on the next page are based on the hexatonic fingerings above.

Ex. 20

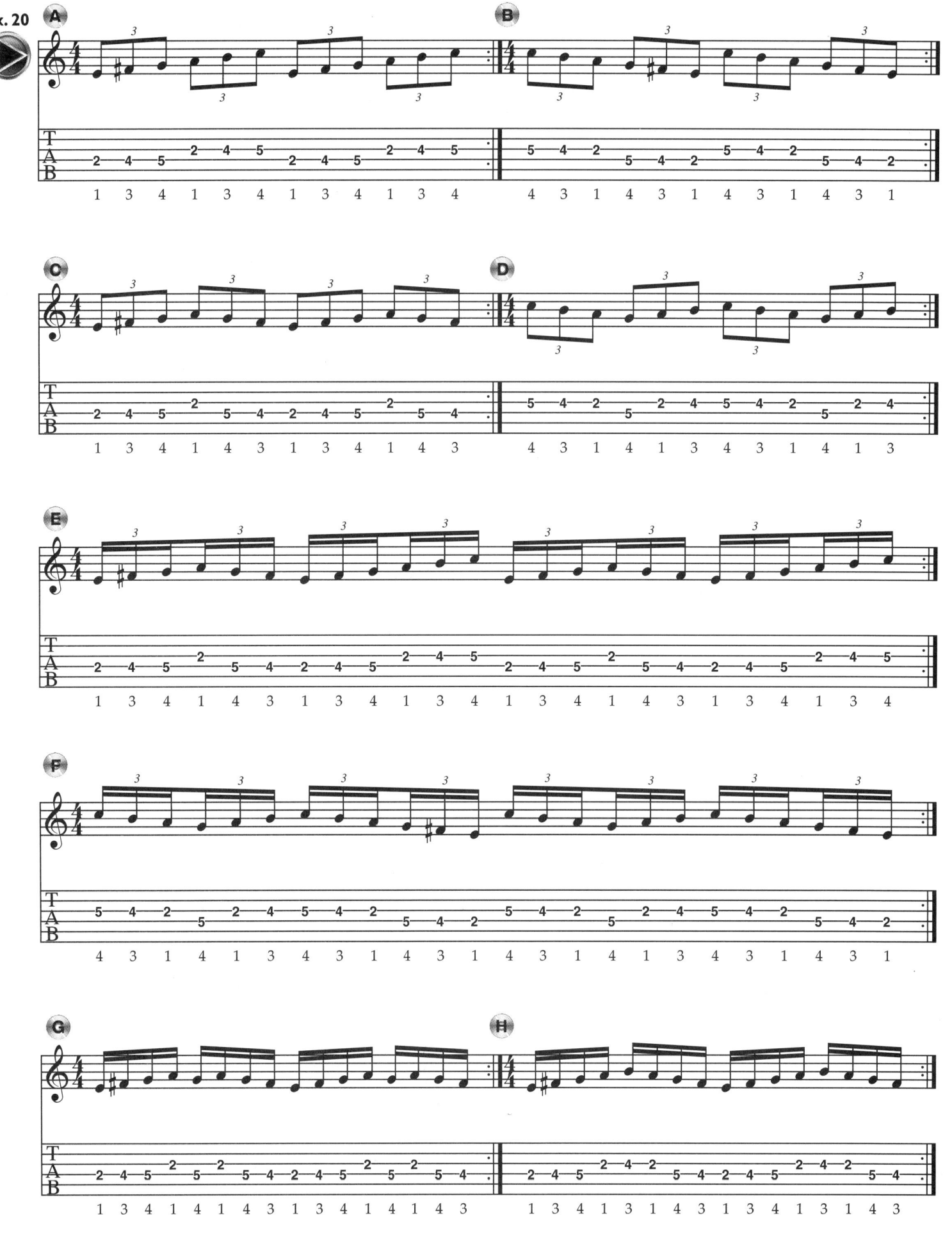

28 — Shredding Guitar Workout

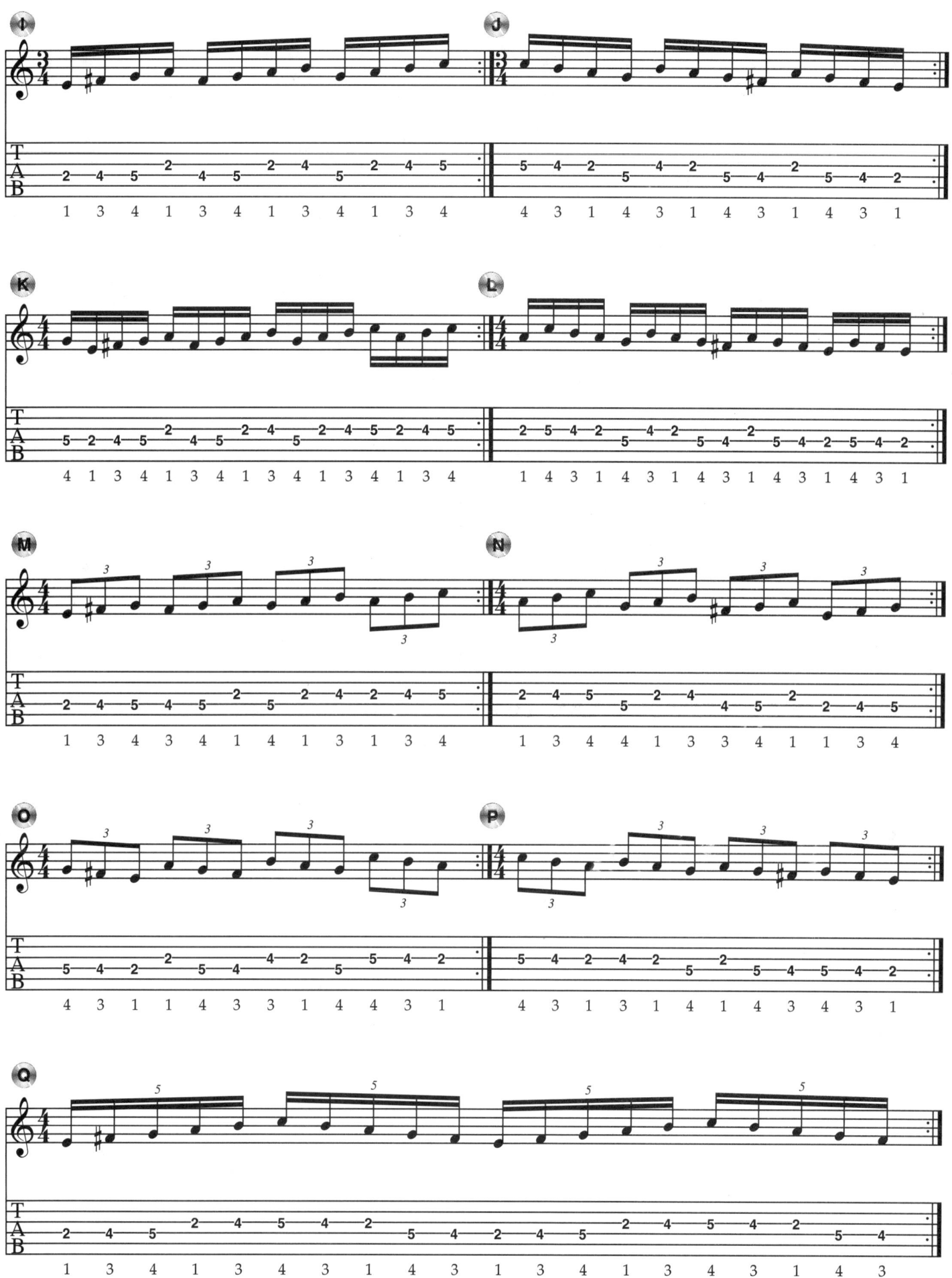

Shredding Guitar Workout

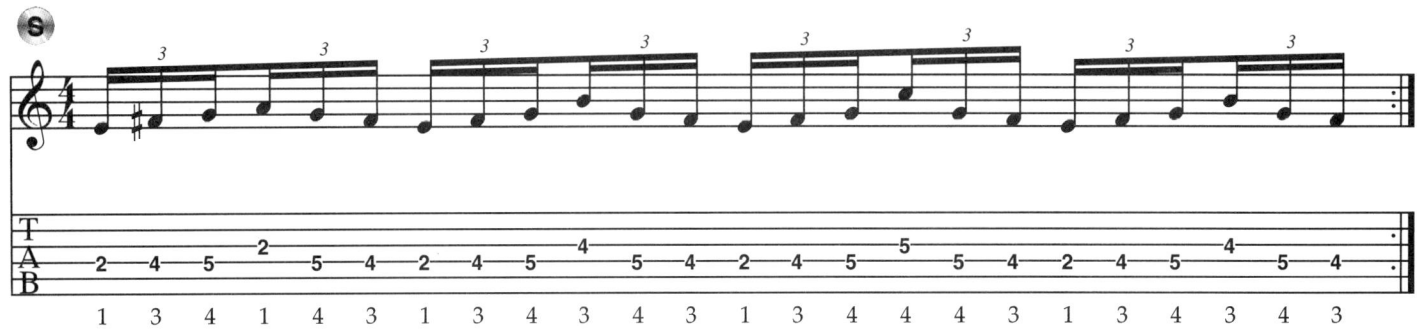

Three-Note-per-String Scales

Now that we have explored the most common patterns on one and two strings, let's take a look at the complete six-string scales. Below are diagrams showing the seven different scale positions, as they relate to the key and scale of C Major. The names only indicate the starting points of each fingering and do not imply an actual modal sound.

Practice and memorize all of these scale positions and then move them to different keys.

F Lydian

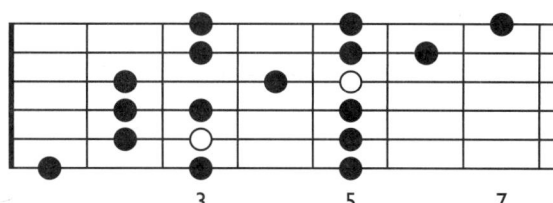

G Mixolydian

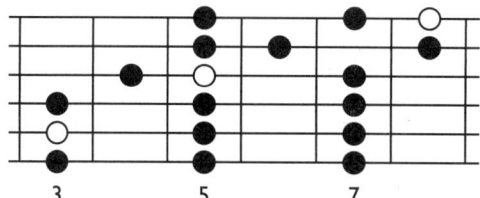

A Aeolian (Natural Minor)

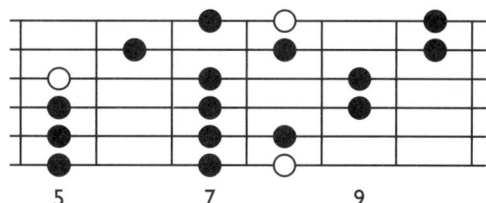

B Locrian

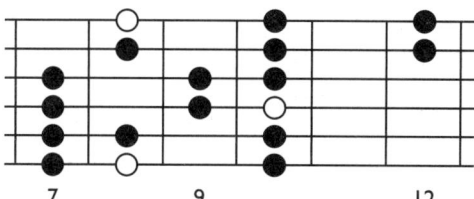

C Ionian (Major)

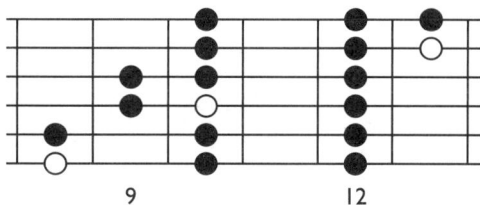

D Dorian

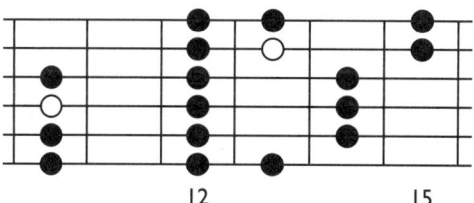

E Phrygian

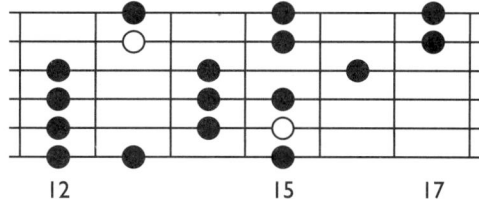

Major Scale Melodic Patterns

The following major scale patterns are in three-, four-, and six-note groupings, and they are in the key of A Major/F# Minor. Use strict alternate picking, and practice these slowly at first with a metronome.

Three-Note Groupings

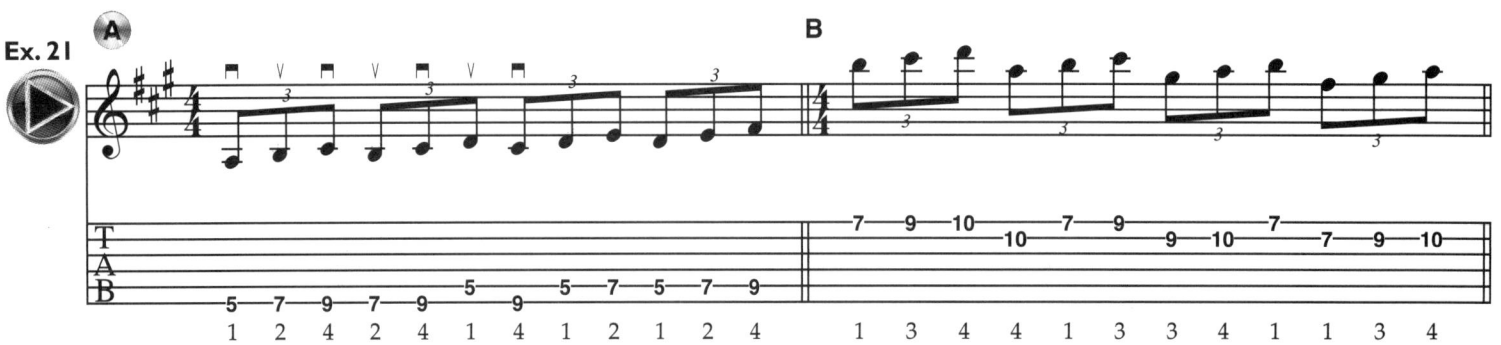

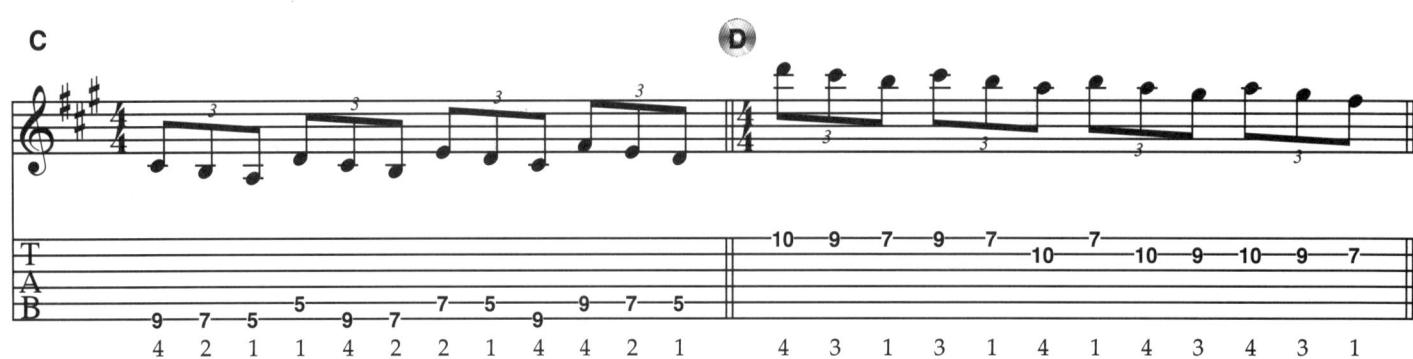

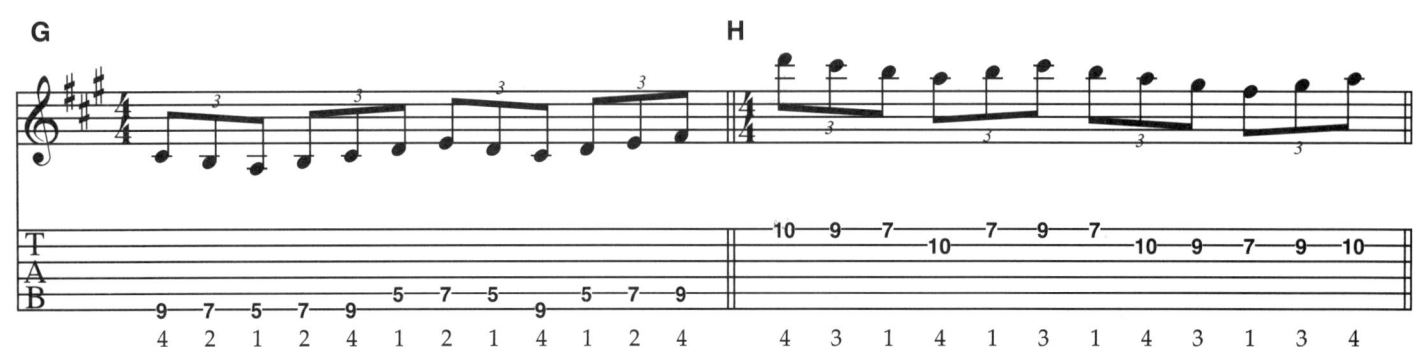

Four-Note Groupings

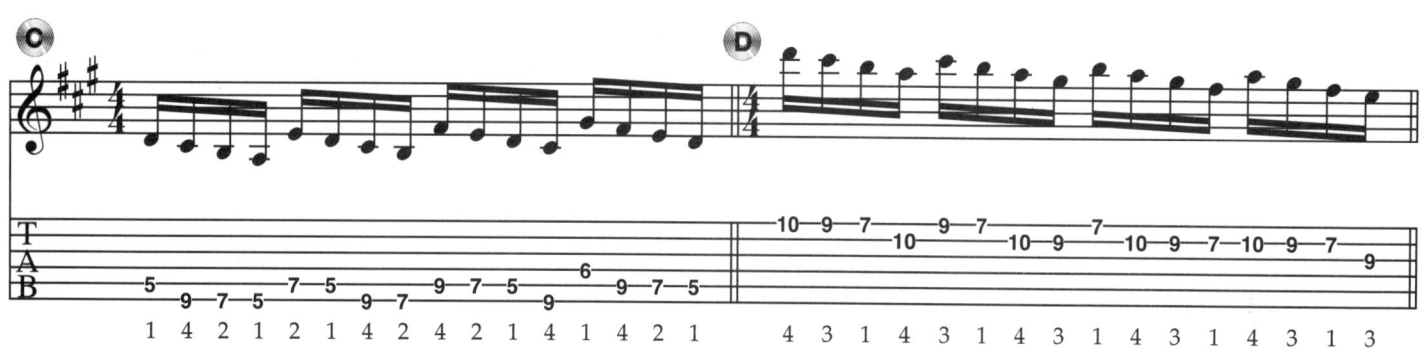
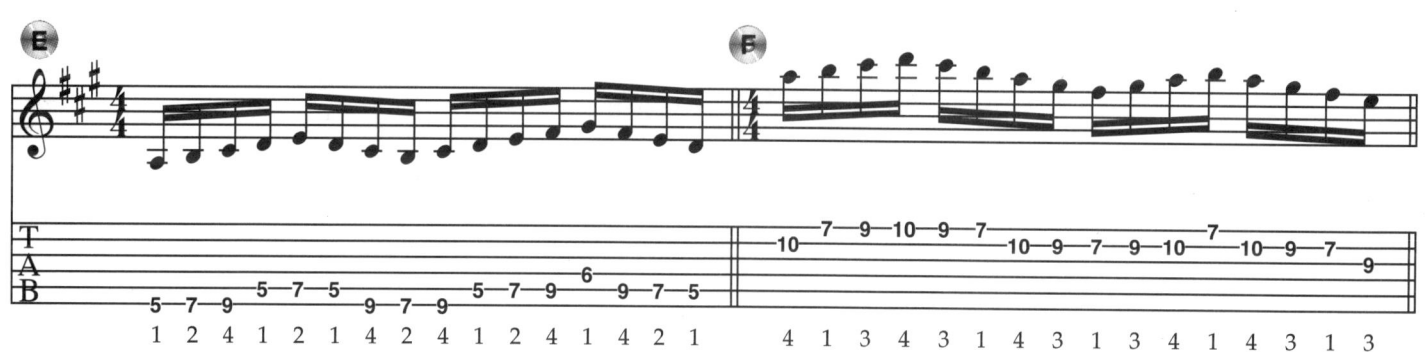
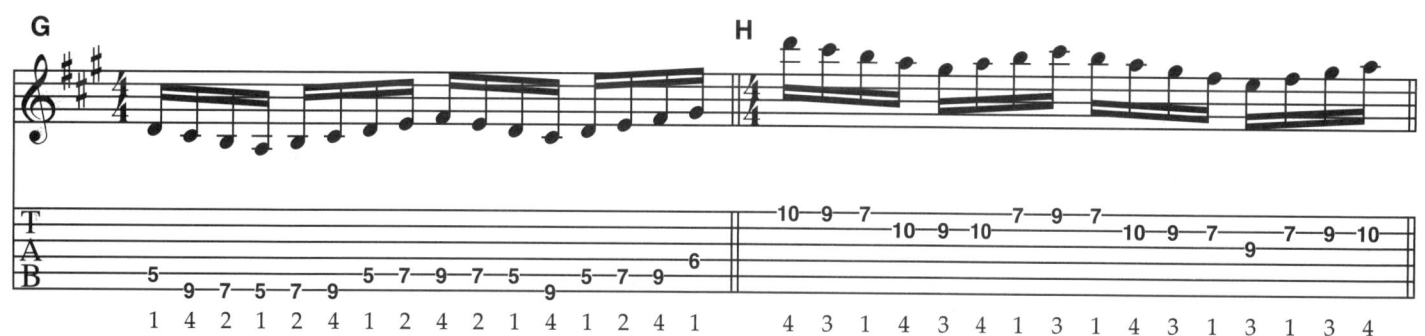

Shredding Guitar Workout

Six-Note Groupings

Ex. 23

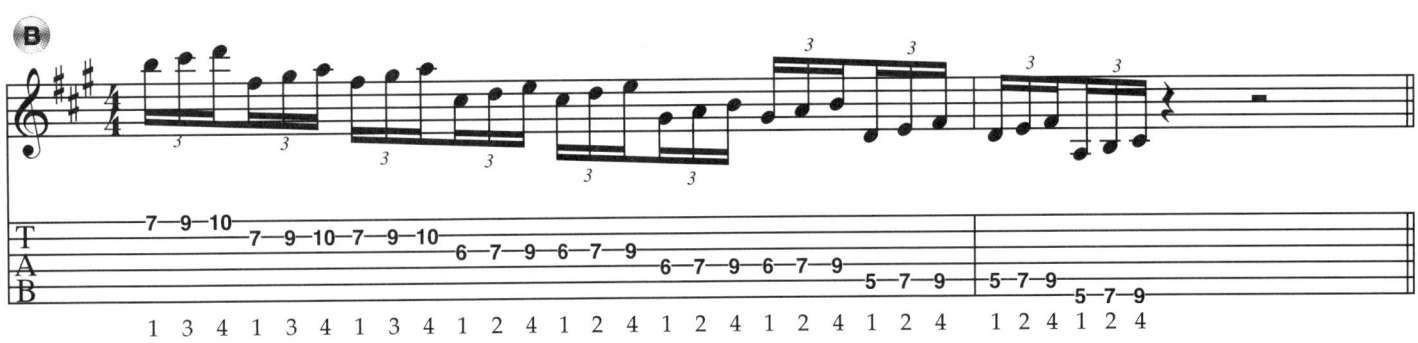

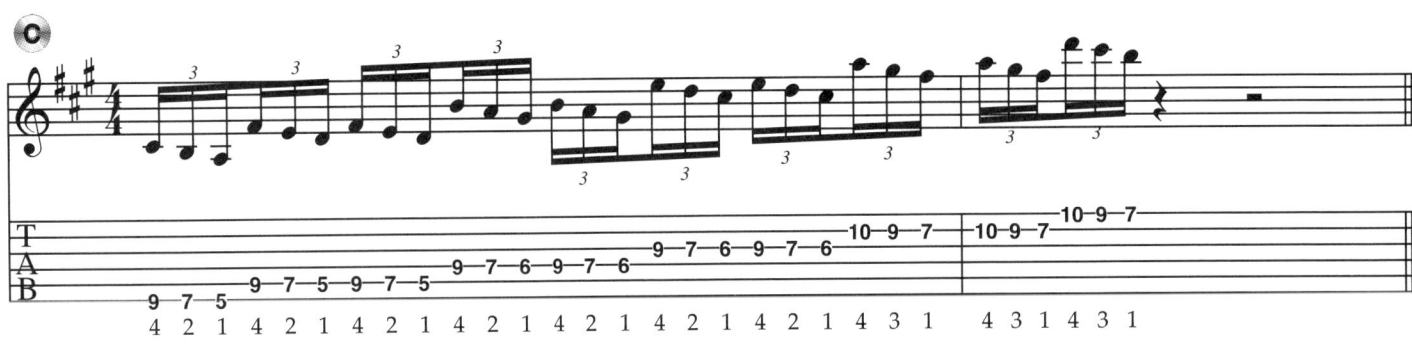

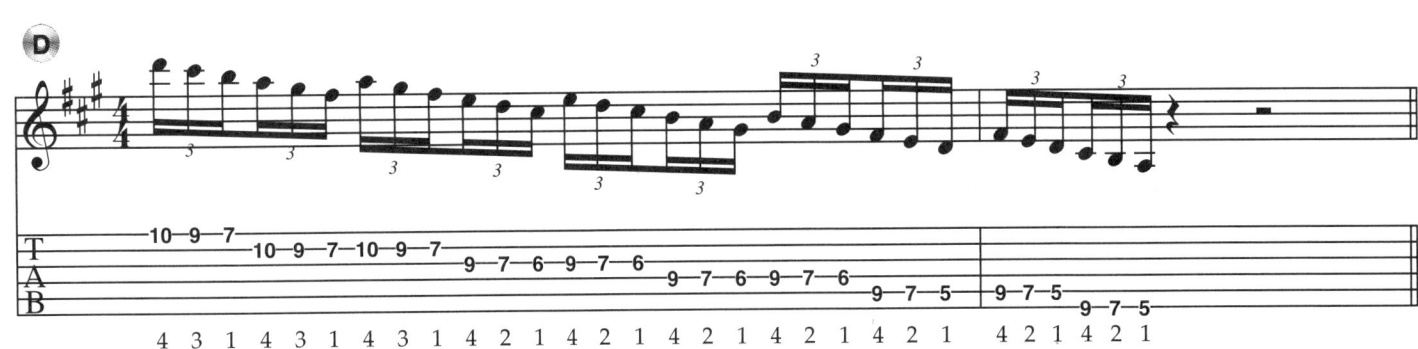

Major Scale Patterns Using Intervals

Another great way to practice your alternate picking is to play different interval patterns within the three-note-per-string scale. We'll base our patterns on 2nds, 3rds, 4ths, 5ths, 6ths, 7ths, and octaves.

4ths

Ex. 26

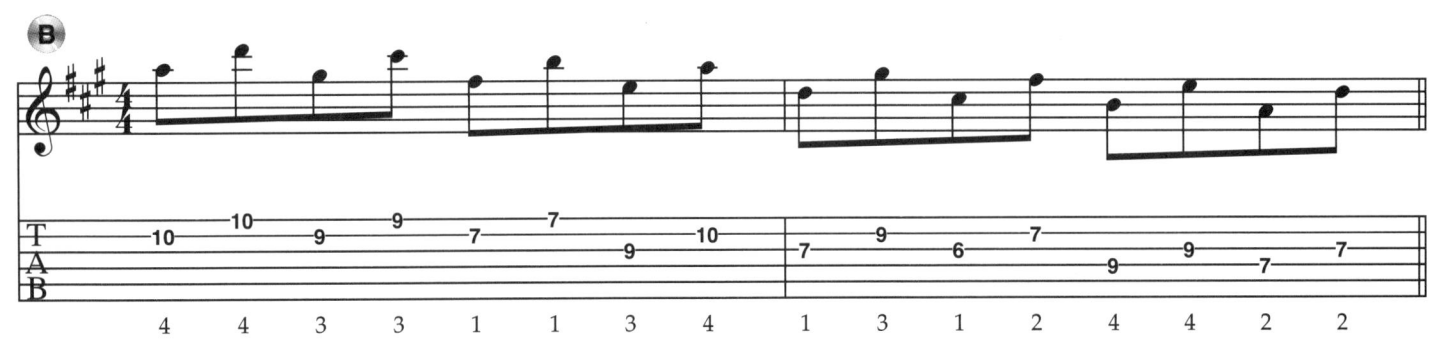

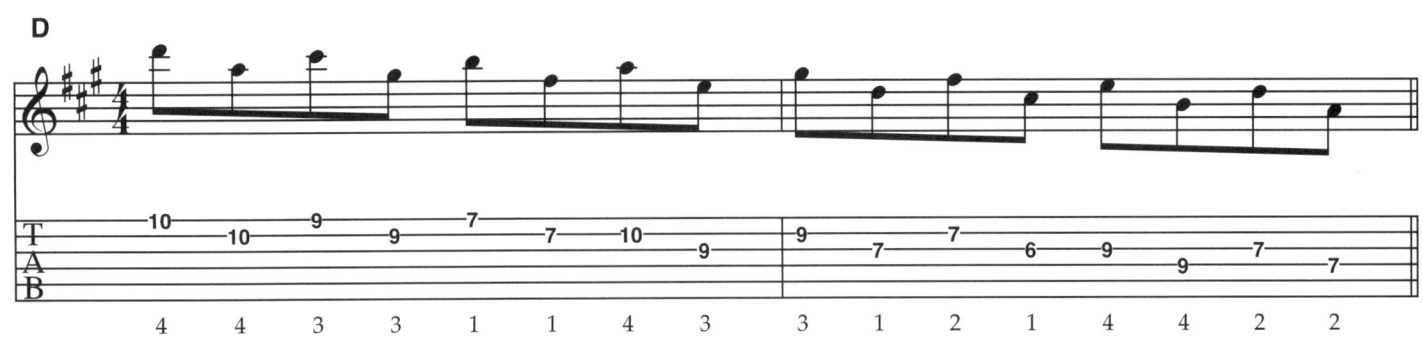

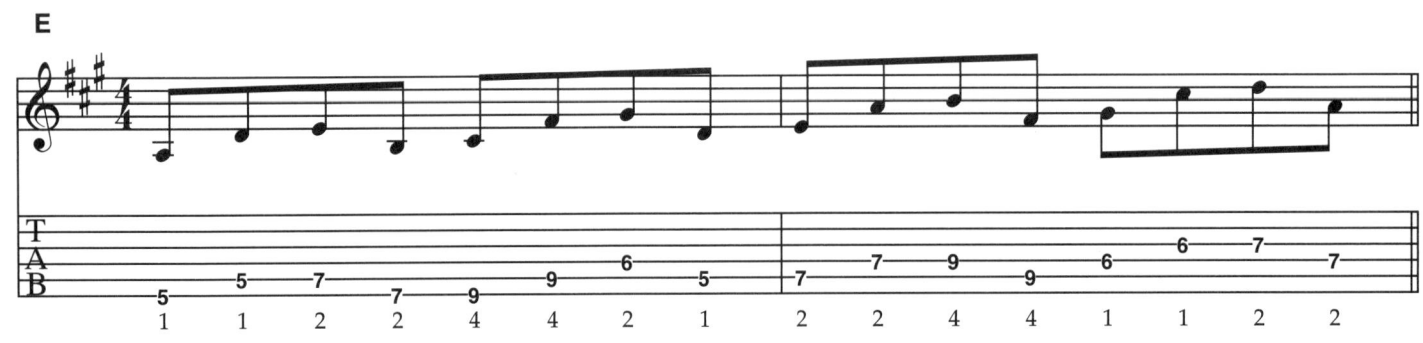

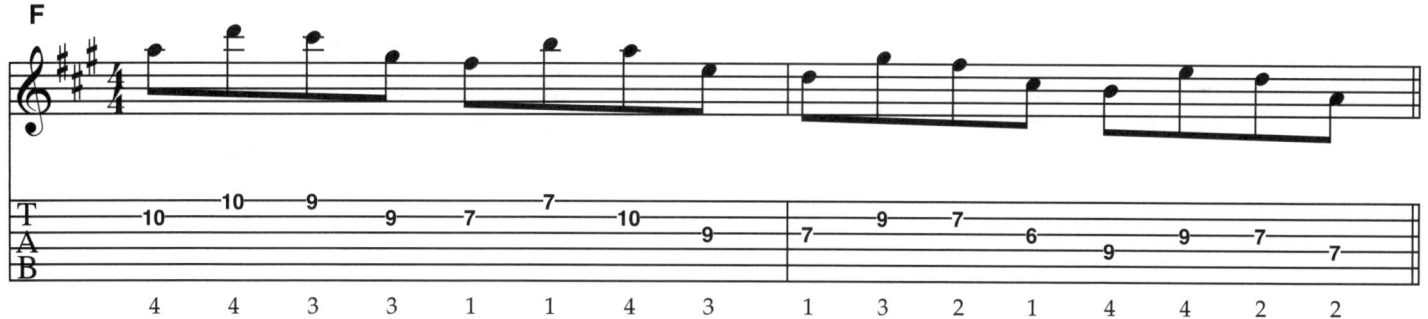

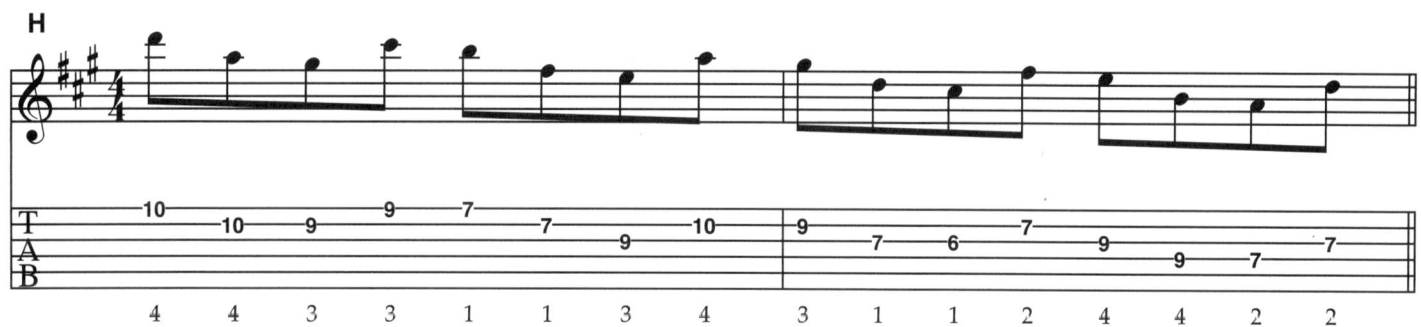

Shredding Guitar Workout — 37

5ths

Ex. 27

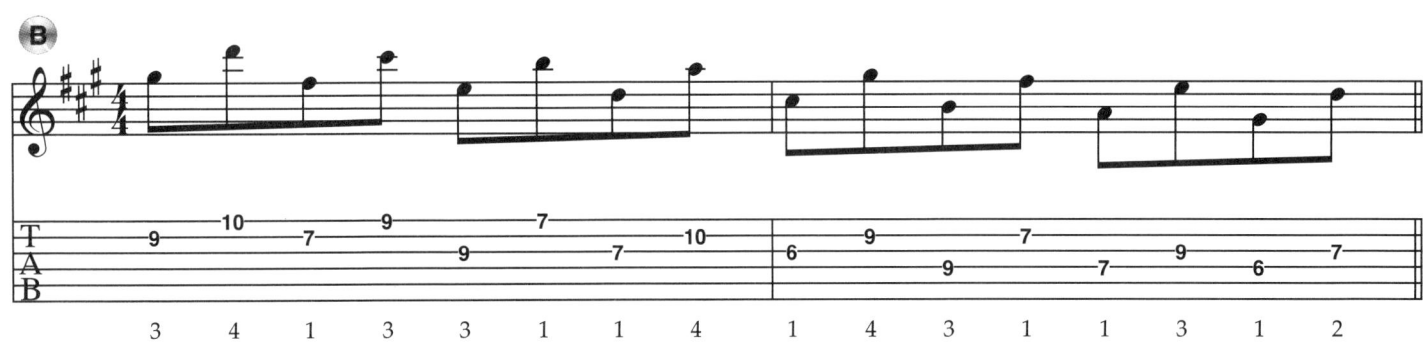

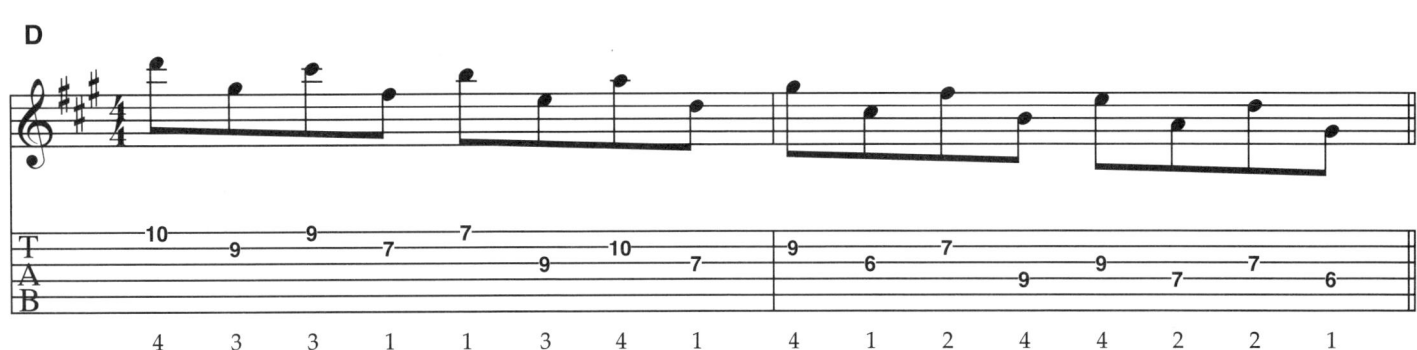

F

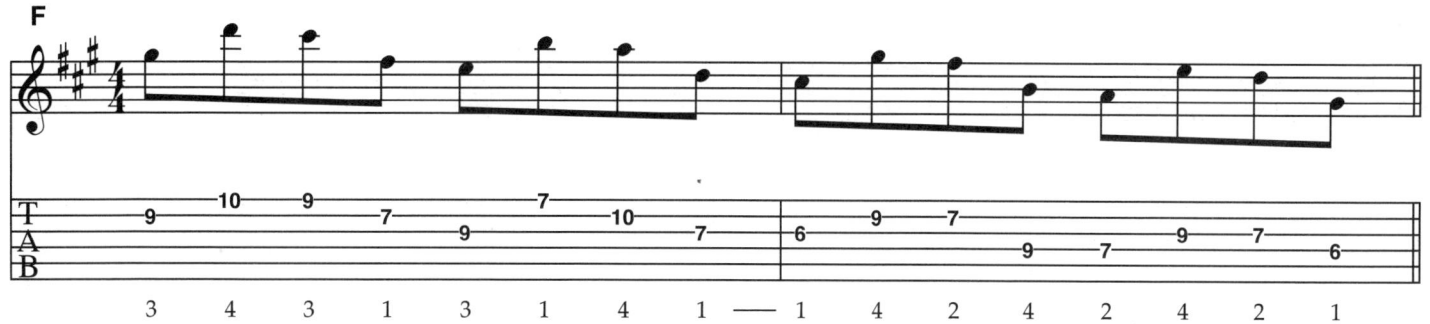

G

H

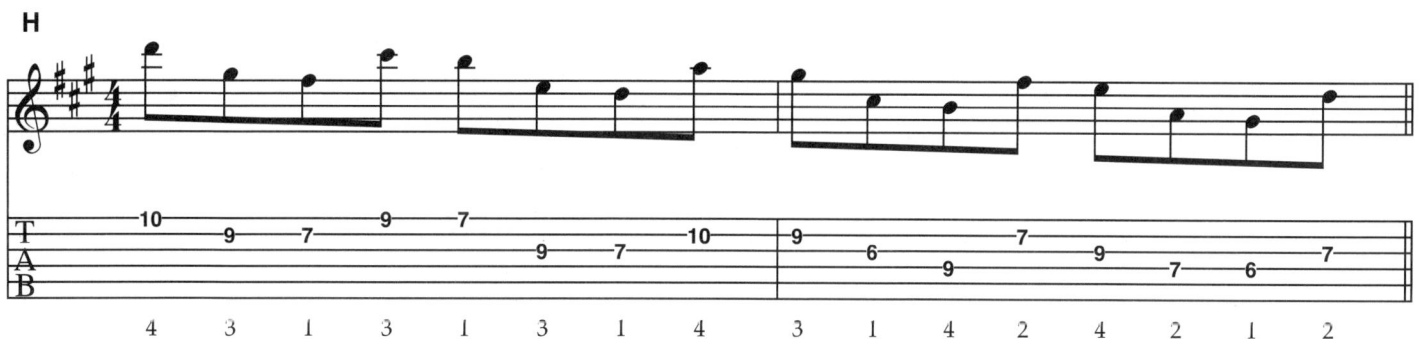

Shredding Guitar Workout

6ths

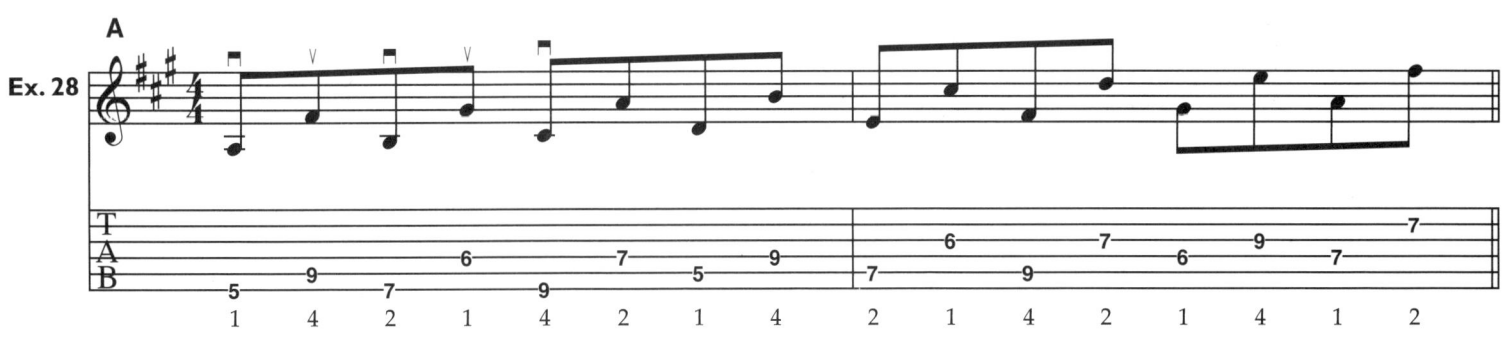
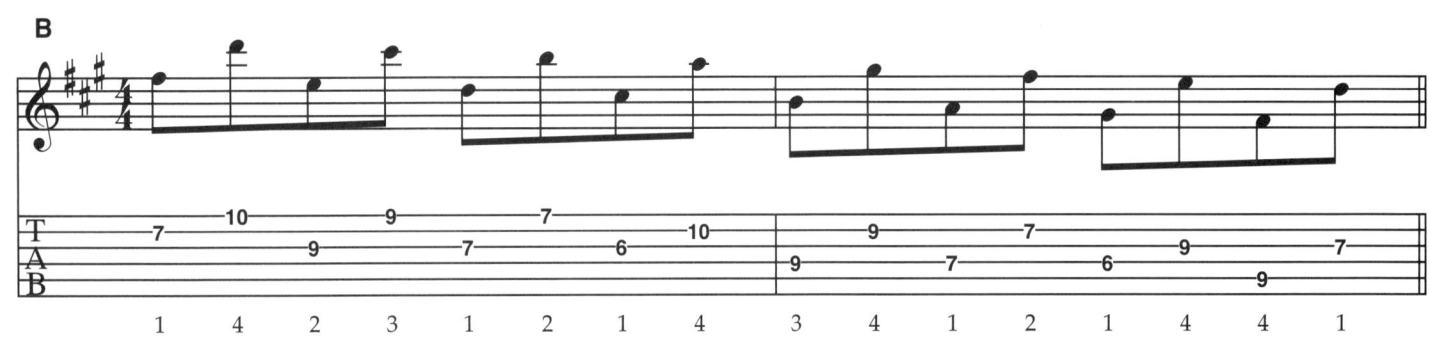
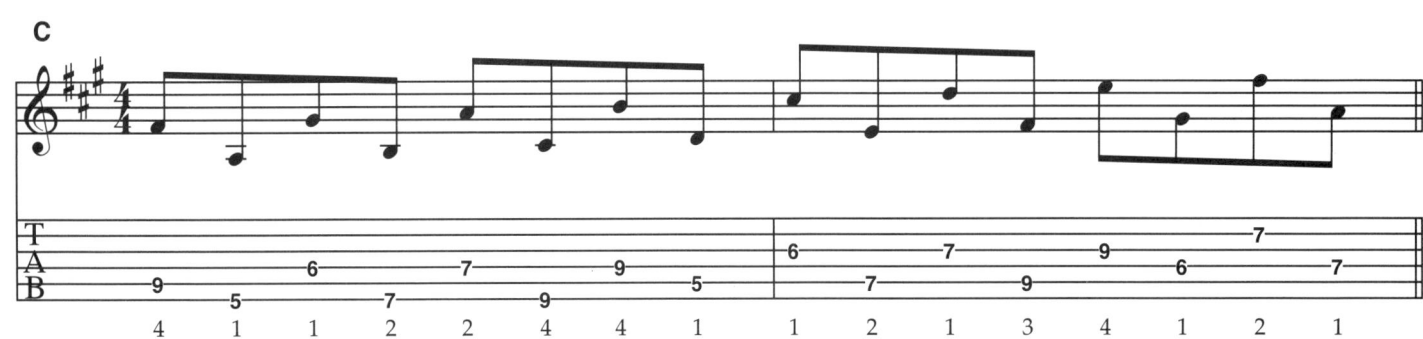
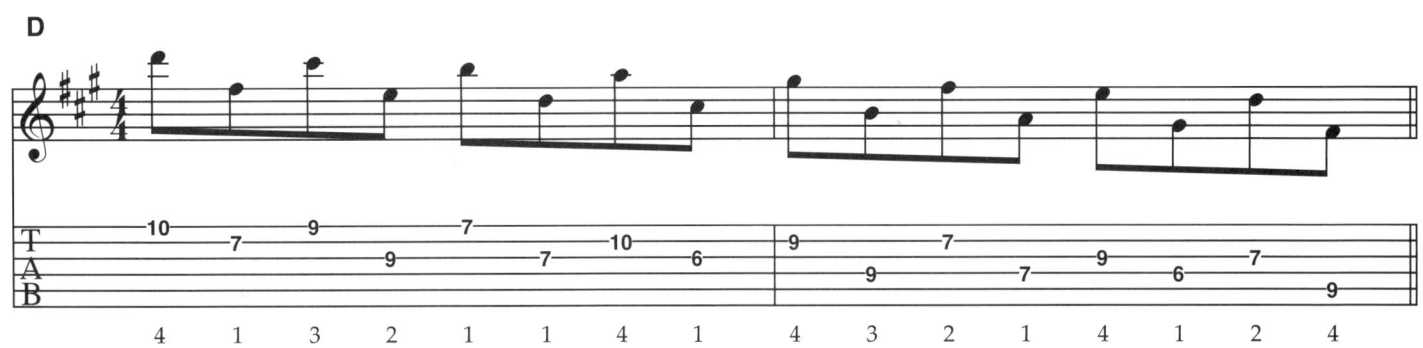

F

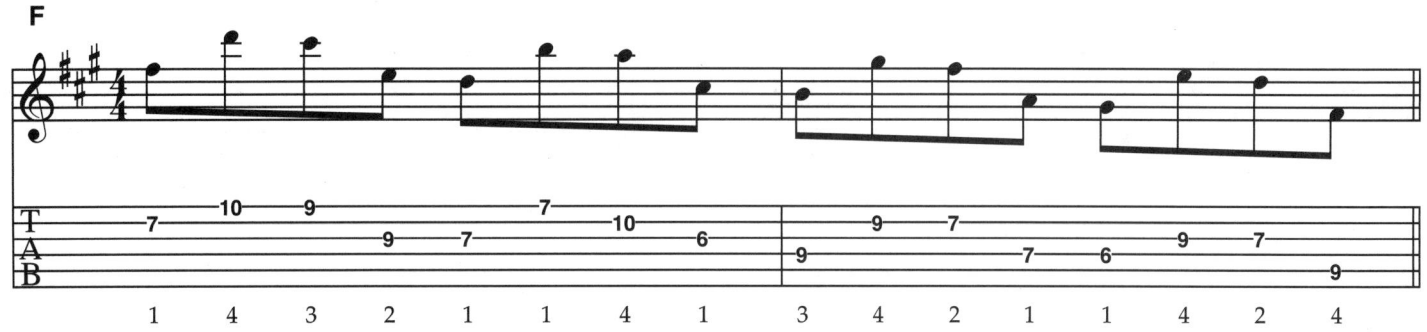

G

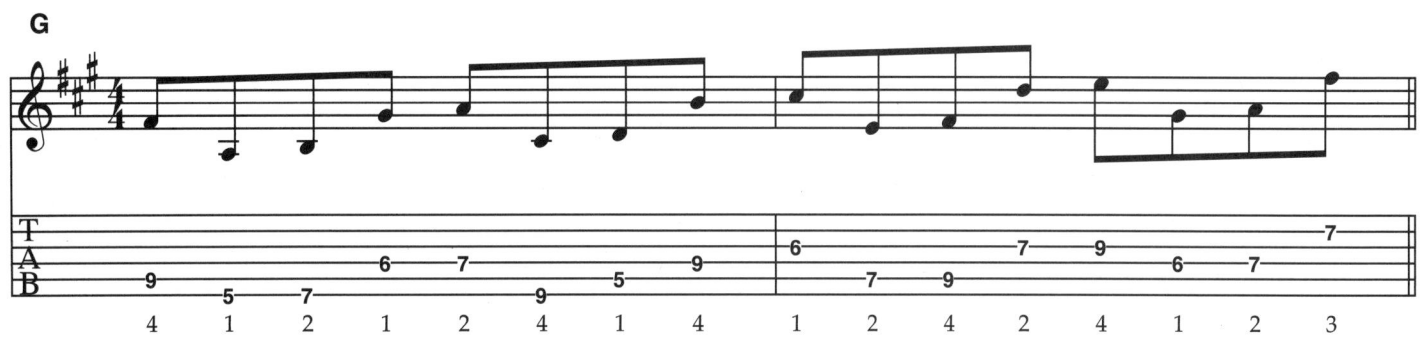

H

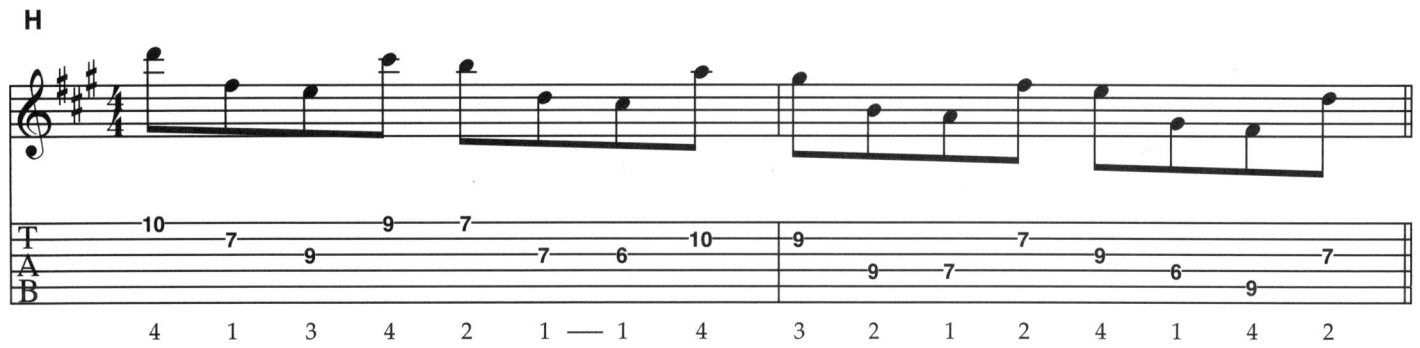

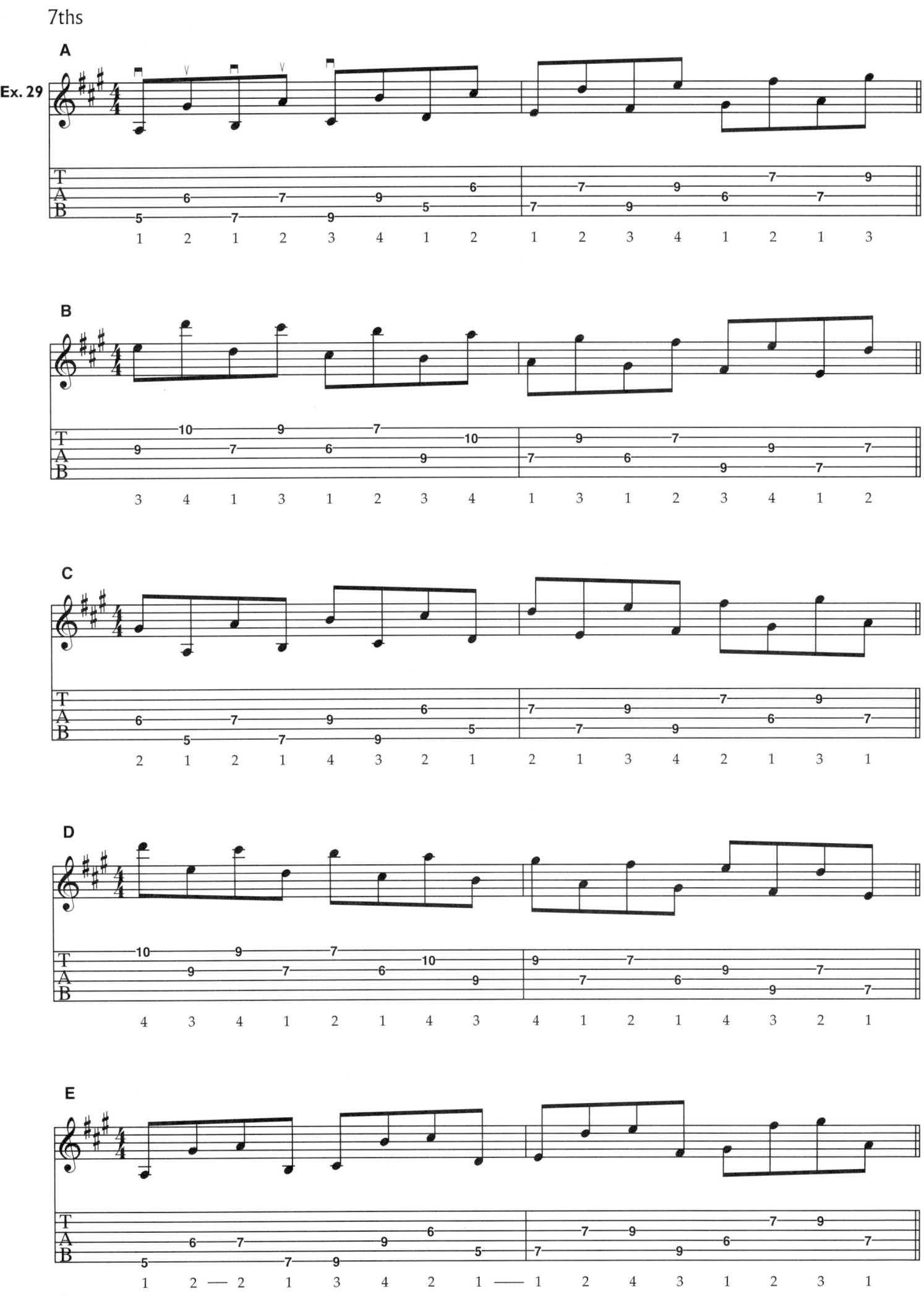

F

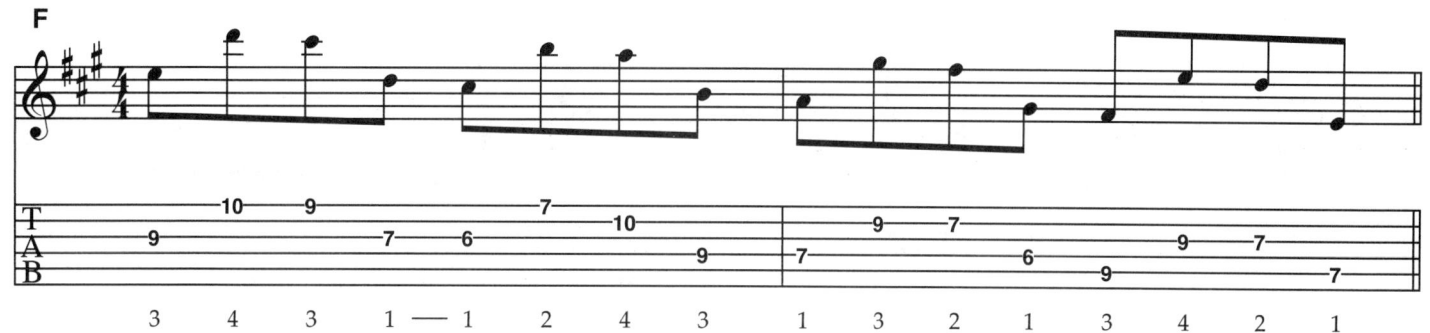

G

H

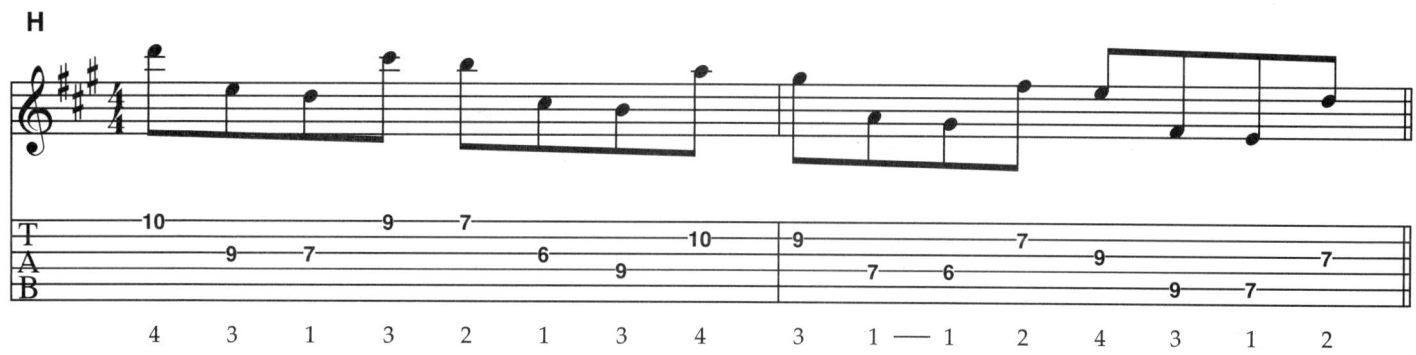

Octaves

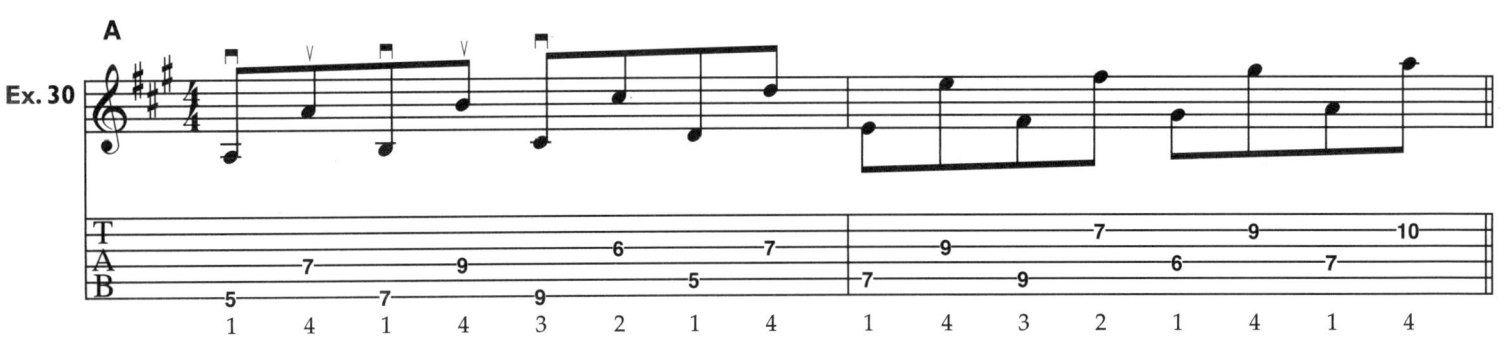

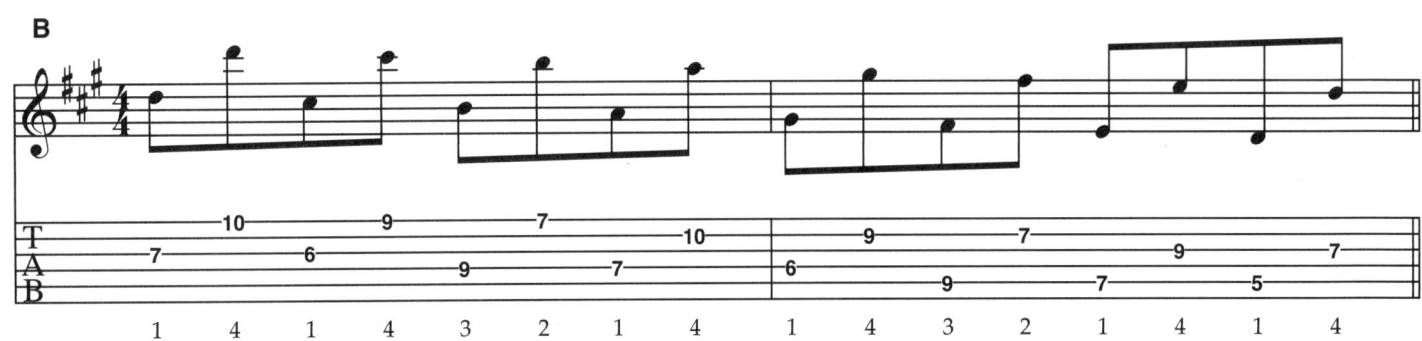

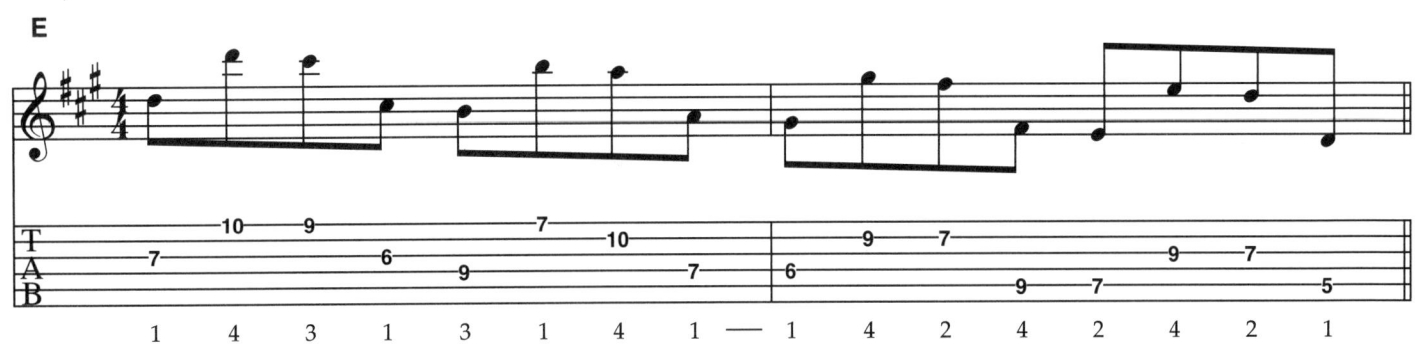

F

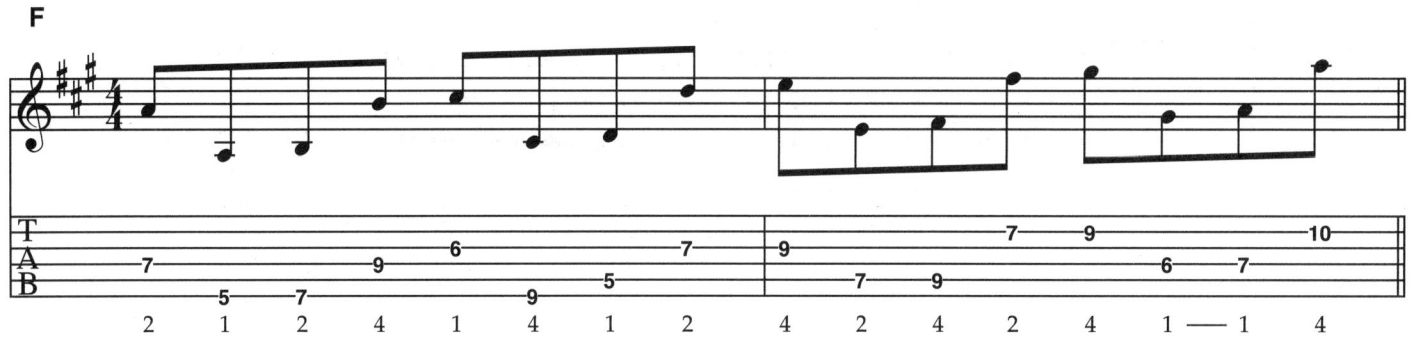

G

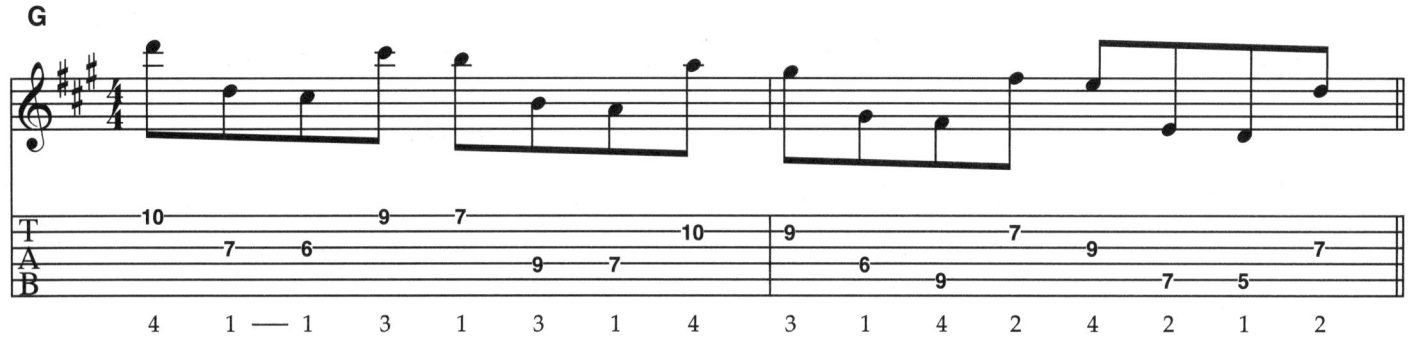

SHREDDING GUITAR WORKOUT — 45

Major Scale Patterns Using Arpeggios

You can also use a scale to play arpeggios and outline chords. The following examples are ascending and descending progressions of triad, 7th-chord, and 9th-chord arpeggios. All of these examples are in the key of A Major (using a variety of keys will help you better understand new concepts) and should be played using strict alternate picking.

Triads

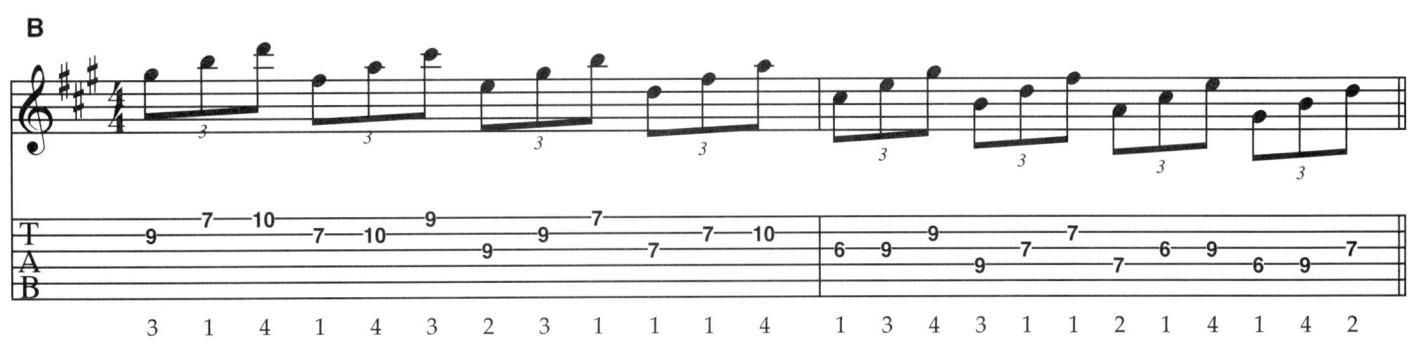

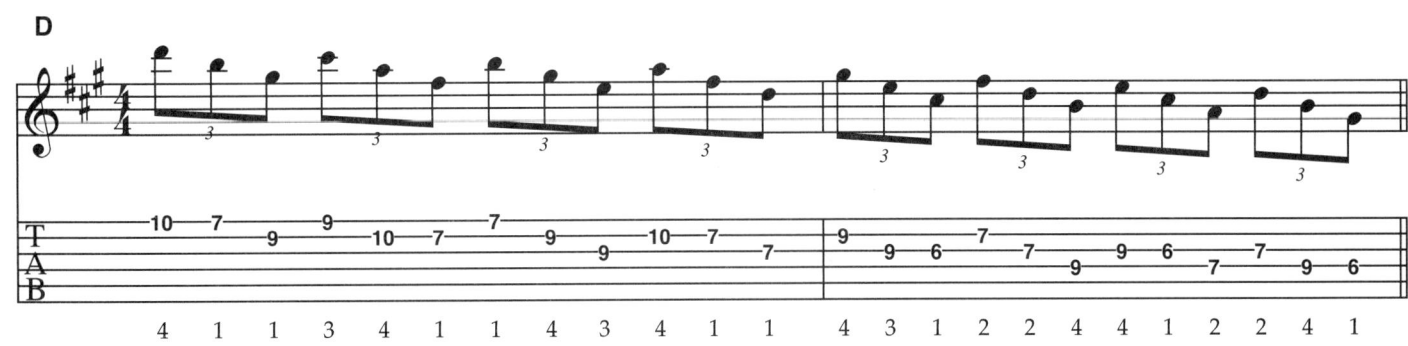

E
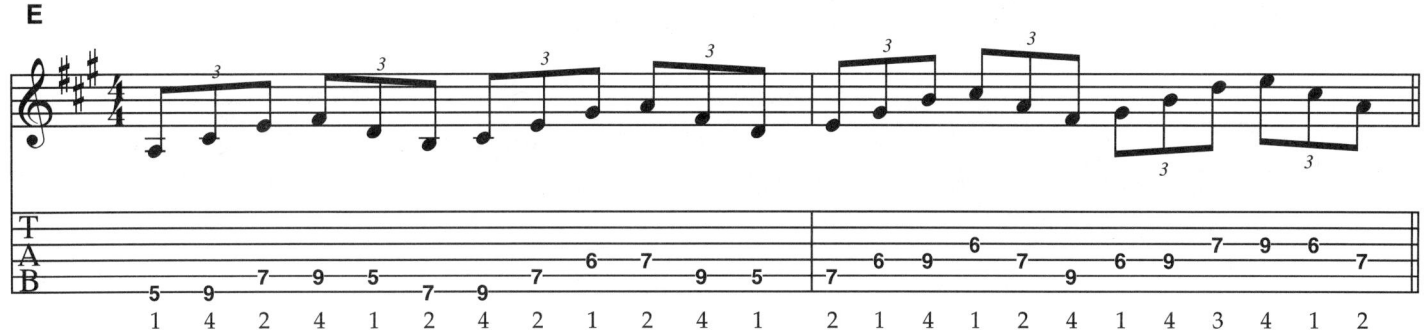

F
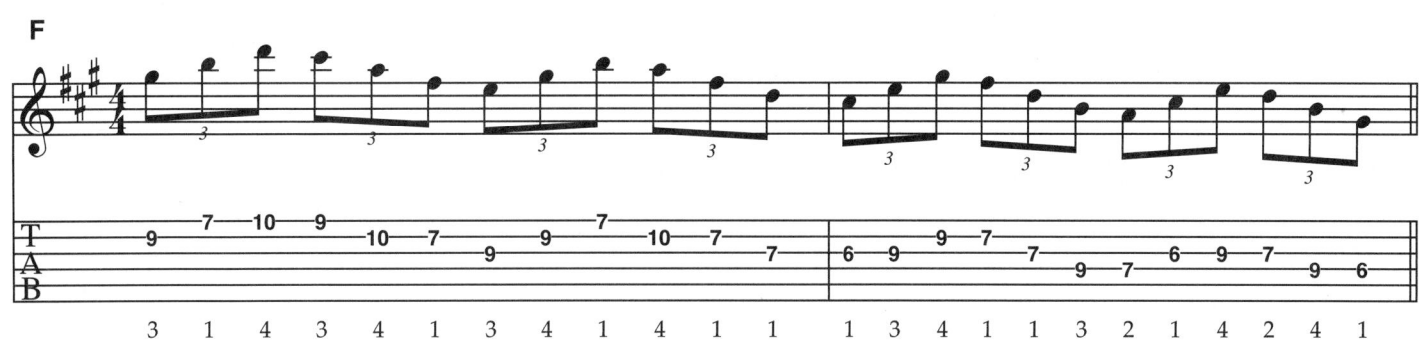

G
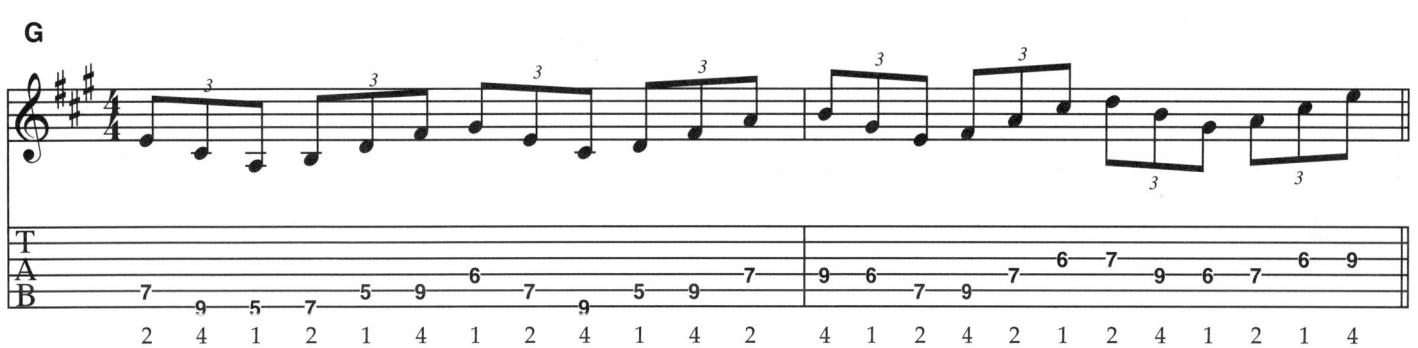

H
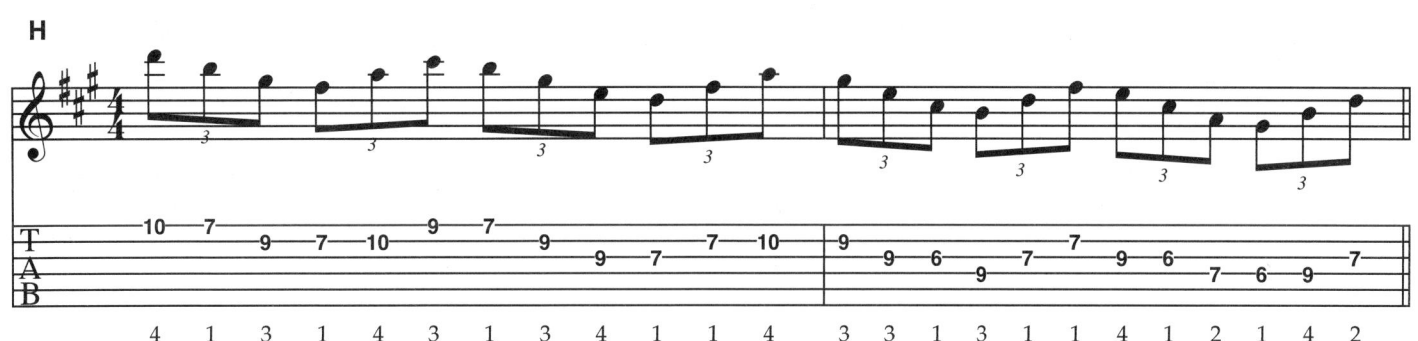

Shredding Guitar Workout

7th Chords

Ex. 32

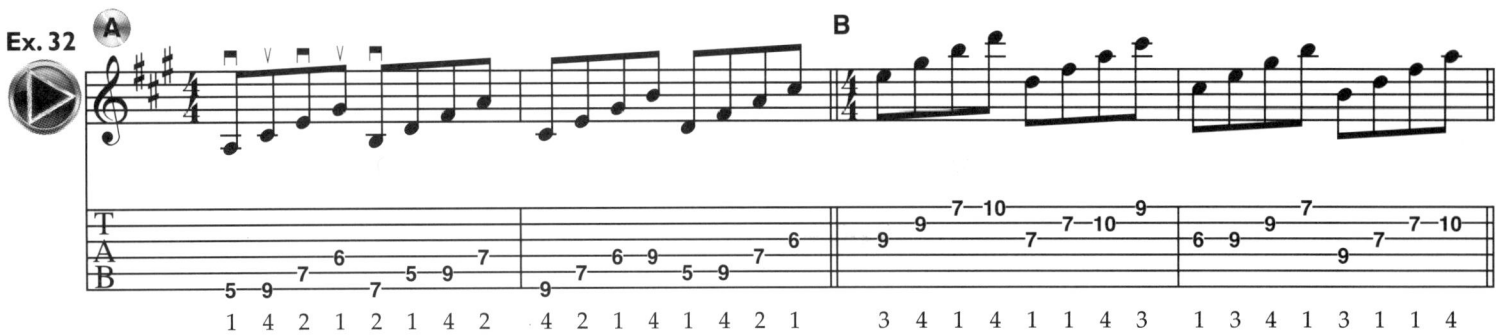

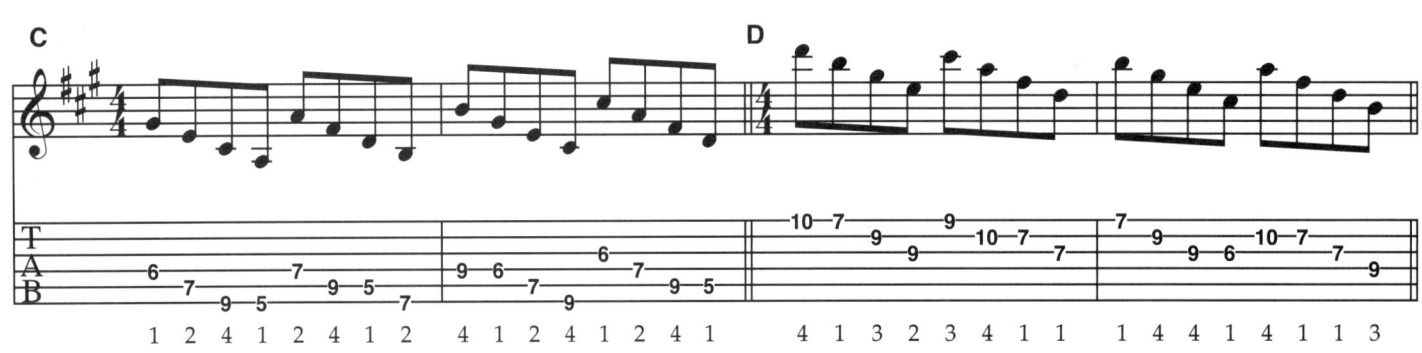

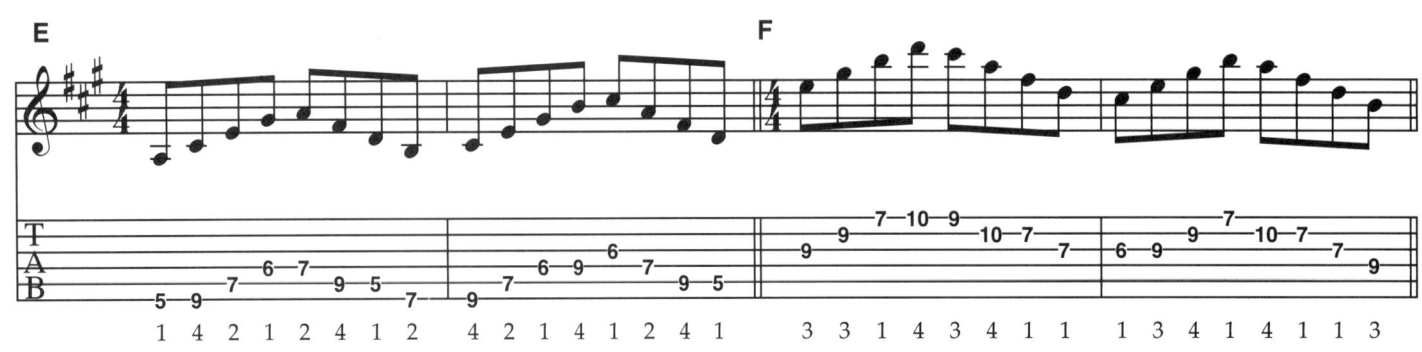

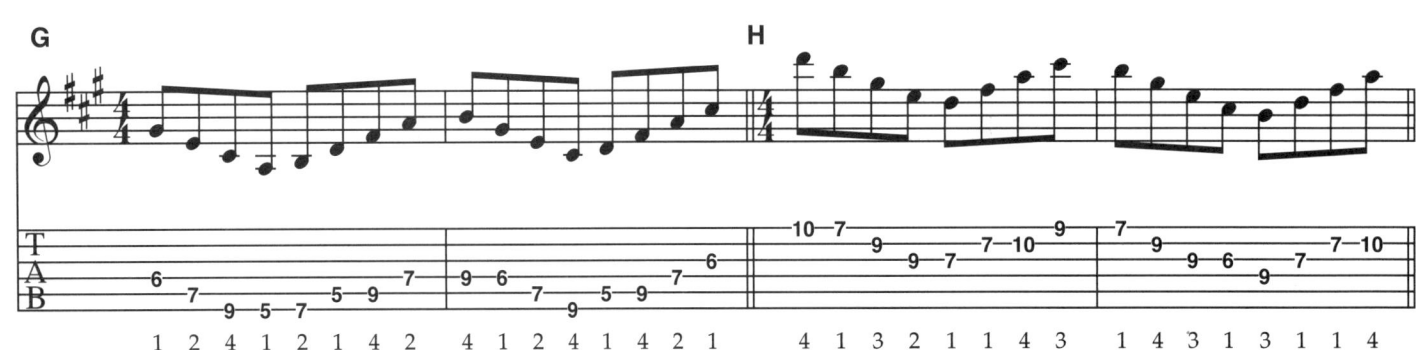

9th Chords

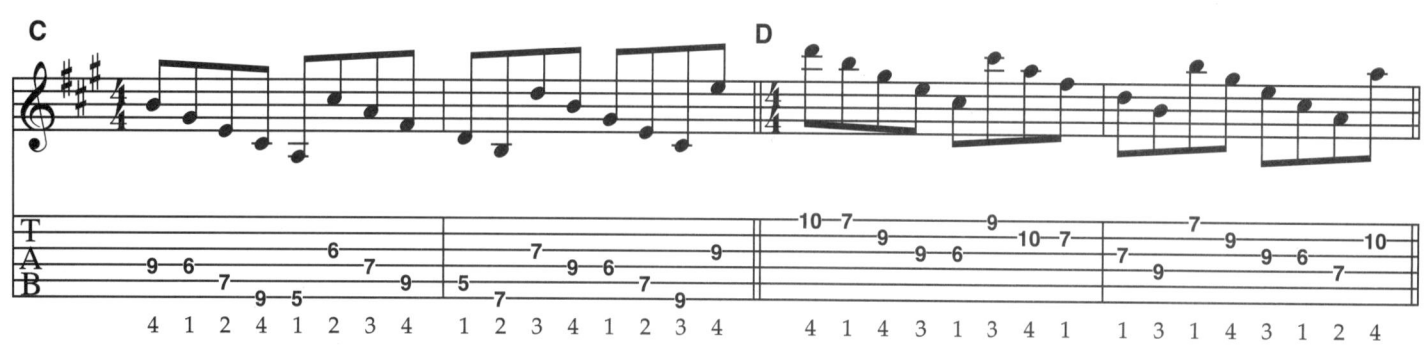

SHREDDING GUITAR WORKOUT

Three-Note-per-String Fingerings for the Seven-String Guitar

Modern guitar playing has brought many changes, including the use of seven-string guitars—and all the exercises we've covered can be adapted for seven-string playing. The diagrams below demonstrate the three-note-per-string scale positions adapted for the seven-string guitar. As you can see, the basic three- and six-note shapes remain the same. If you have a seven-string guitar, try to extend the scale patterns across the entire fretboard.

C Ionian
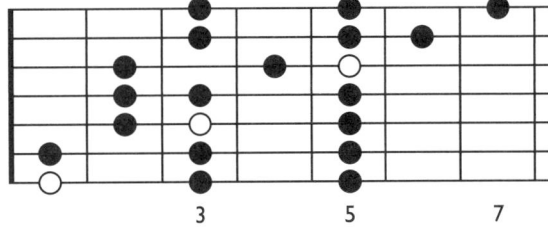

D Dorian
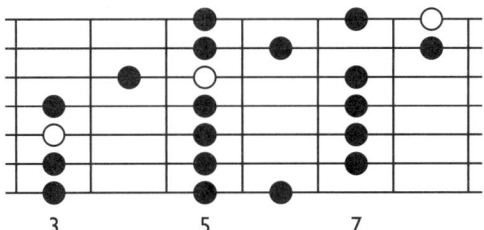

E Phrygian
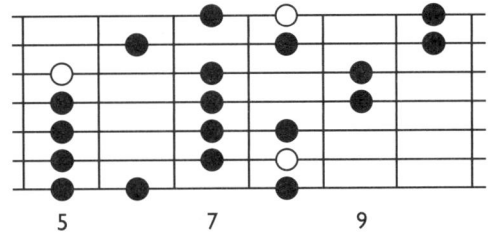

F Lydian
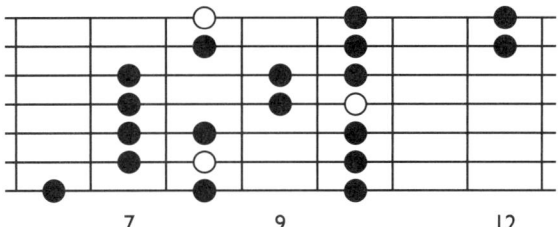

G Mixolydian
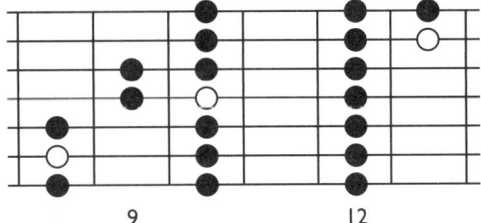

A Aeolian
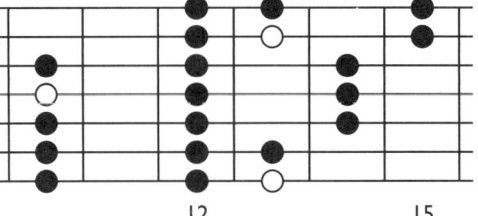

B Locrian
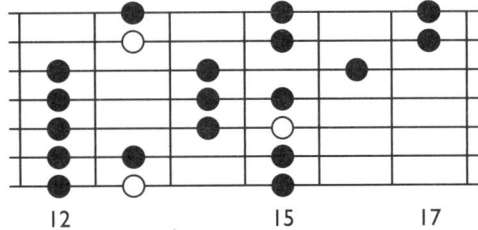

Speed Development

Speed, coordination, and stamina are important to rock guitar soloing and shredding. To shred successfully, you need to train like an athlete. There are several different approaches for gaining speed and control.

Approach 1

One way is to understand a lick's rhythm and be able to play it in different rhythmic interpretations. To demonstrate how this works, check out Example 34A below. There, we have a simple ascending triplet pattern, which can be played as three notes per beat or as six notes per beat. This requires you to perceive a rhythmic structure and be able to play it with a full- or half-time feel. Set your metronome to a reasonable tempo, like 100 BPM (beats per minute). Practice the phrase as eighth-note triplets for one or two measures, then double up the feel to sixteenth-note sextuplets. Play this for a few measures and then drop back again to eighth-note triplets. Repeat this as many times as it takes for you to be able to switch back and forth easily. Then, increase the tempo. To practice this idea further, you can use any of the patterns we've already covered.

Approach 2

Another way to develop speed and stamina is to run through different chromatic scales and patterns on your fretboard, increasing the speed after every run through. Don't forget to set the metronome to a reasonable tempo in the beginning, so there is room to increase it. You will find that over time, your baseline speed will rise, as will your top speed. Try to move in small increments, like 8–12 beats per minute, when moving up the metronome settings. Make sure everything is synchronized and played cleanly. If it feels like you are losing coordination, back off a few beats per minute and find your tempo. For a while, this will be the speed at which you're comfortable playing. It is important to be able to play fast easily and comfortably, without overextending your physical abilities.

Ex. 35

Ex. 36

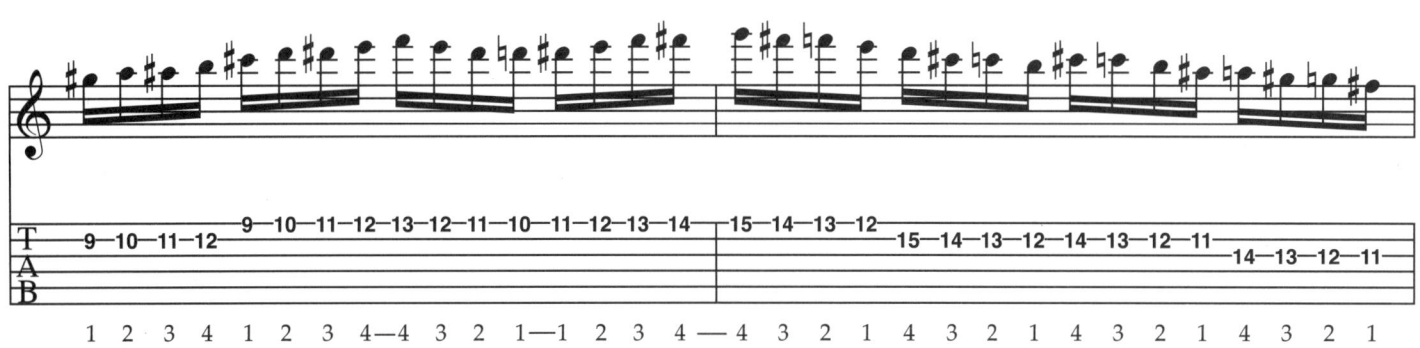
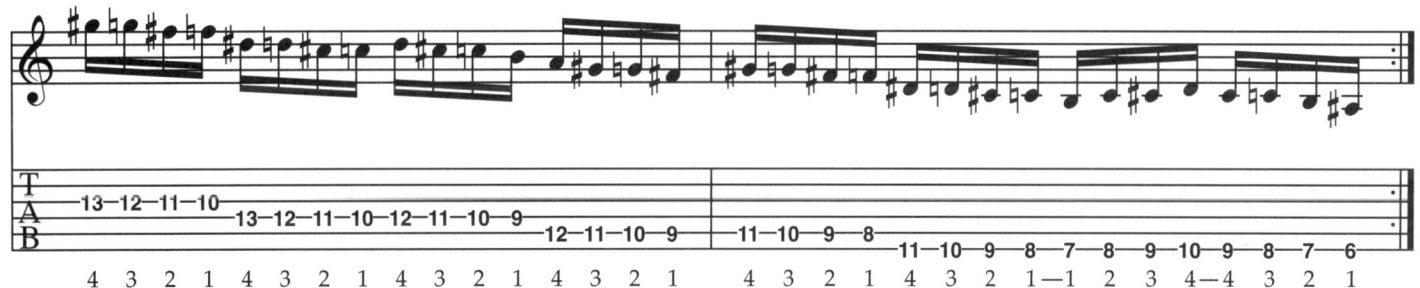

SHREDDING GUITAR WORKOUT — 53

Approach 3

The ultimate test of control and speed is the Rhythm Pyramid exercise. Any exercise, pattern, or scale can be applied to this challenging idea. When first starting, choose a tempo that is not too fast or too slow, then apply the rhythmic idea to the pattern of your choice. In the example on the next page, we are playing an ascending and descending scale pattern. We start off with an eighth-note rhythm, but you could begin with whole notes and then move up to half notes, quarter notes, and so on. This exercise will help you understand the importance of knowing the rhythm in each phrase and how it is connects to your physical playing. The chart below shows how the note values break down in relation to each other. You can refer to this chart when creating your own Rhythm Pyramid.

Rhythm Pyramid

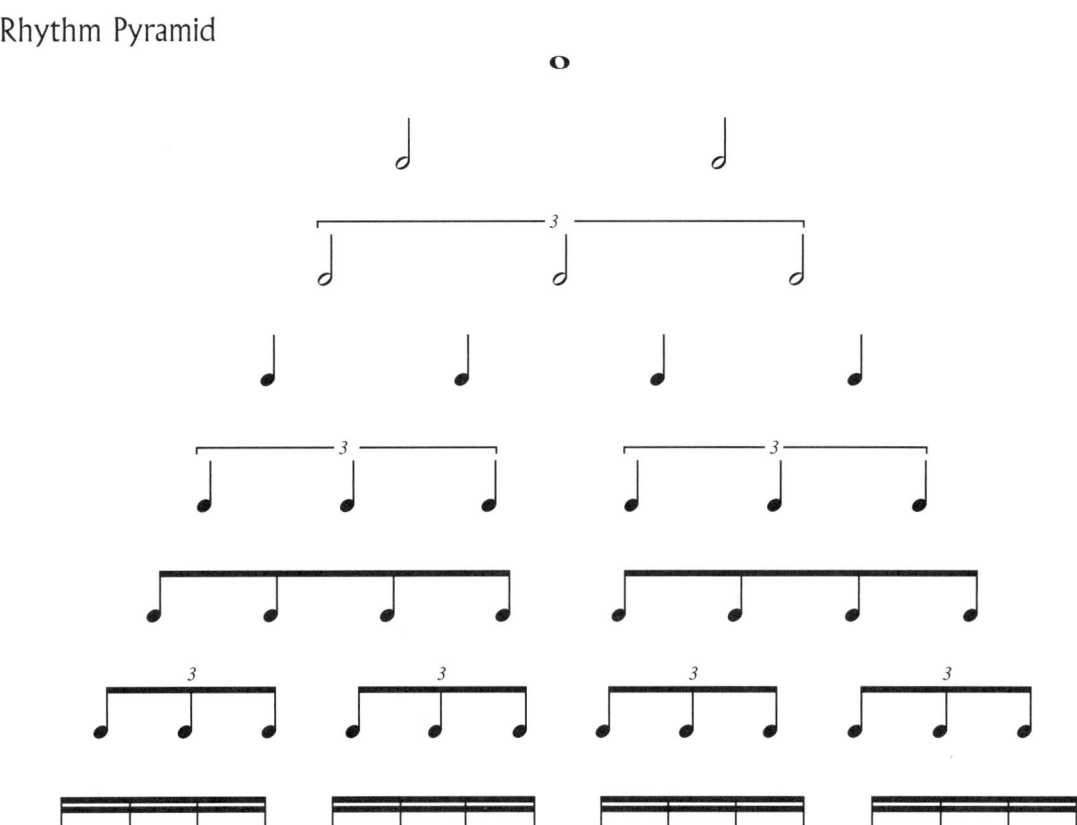

Rhythm Pyramid

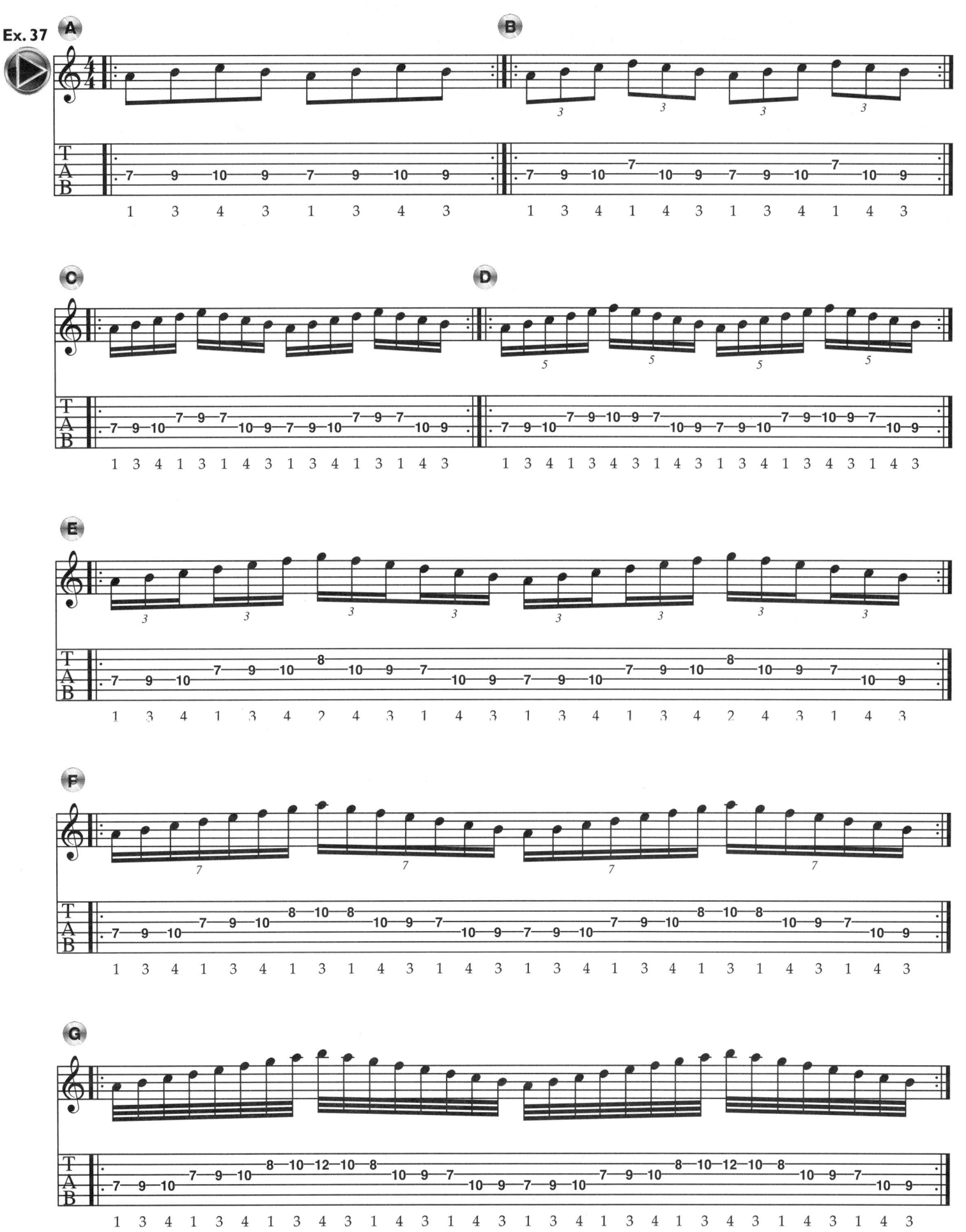

SWEEP PICKING

Sweep picking, or *sweeping*, is a technique commonly used with arpeggios, but it can also be used to play scales. Sweeping utilizes the picking direction, either ascending or descending, to play notes that are located on adjacent strings in one "sweeping" motion. Contrary to alternate picking, sweeping generates a different, more fluid sound and can be used to play passages much faster than with alternate picking. Sweep picking requires accuracy and precise left- and right-hand coordination to produce clean arpeggios and runs. It is important to lift the fretting-hand fingers immediately after each note is played and apply slight muting with the picking hand in order to achieve this.

Ex. 38

The sweeping concept can also be applied to scales by organizing the pick strokes so that the sweep occurs between notes on adjacent strings. This focused type of sweeping is called *economy picking*, and it can be used on any scale that can be organized in even and odd note groupings on each string. Check out the following example of economy picking.

Ex. 39

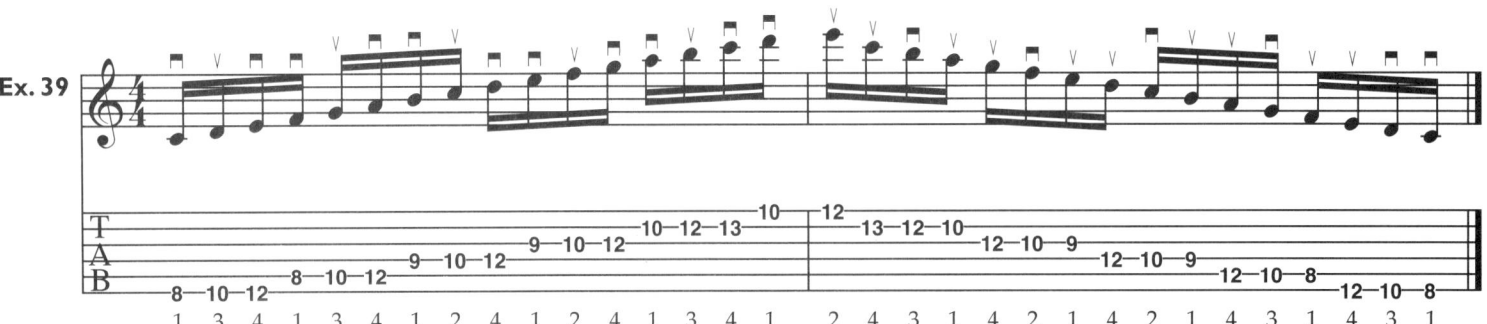

Sweep picking provides a great approach to playing complex musical passages very quickly and precisely. But in order to achieve perfect left- and right-hand synchronization, some basic warm-up exercises are necessary.

The following chromatic exercises will help you develop good sweep-picking technique.

Ex. 40

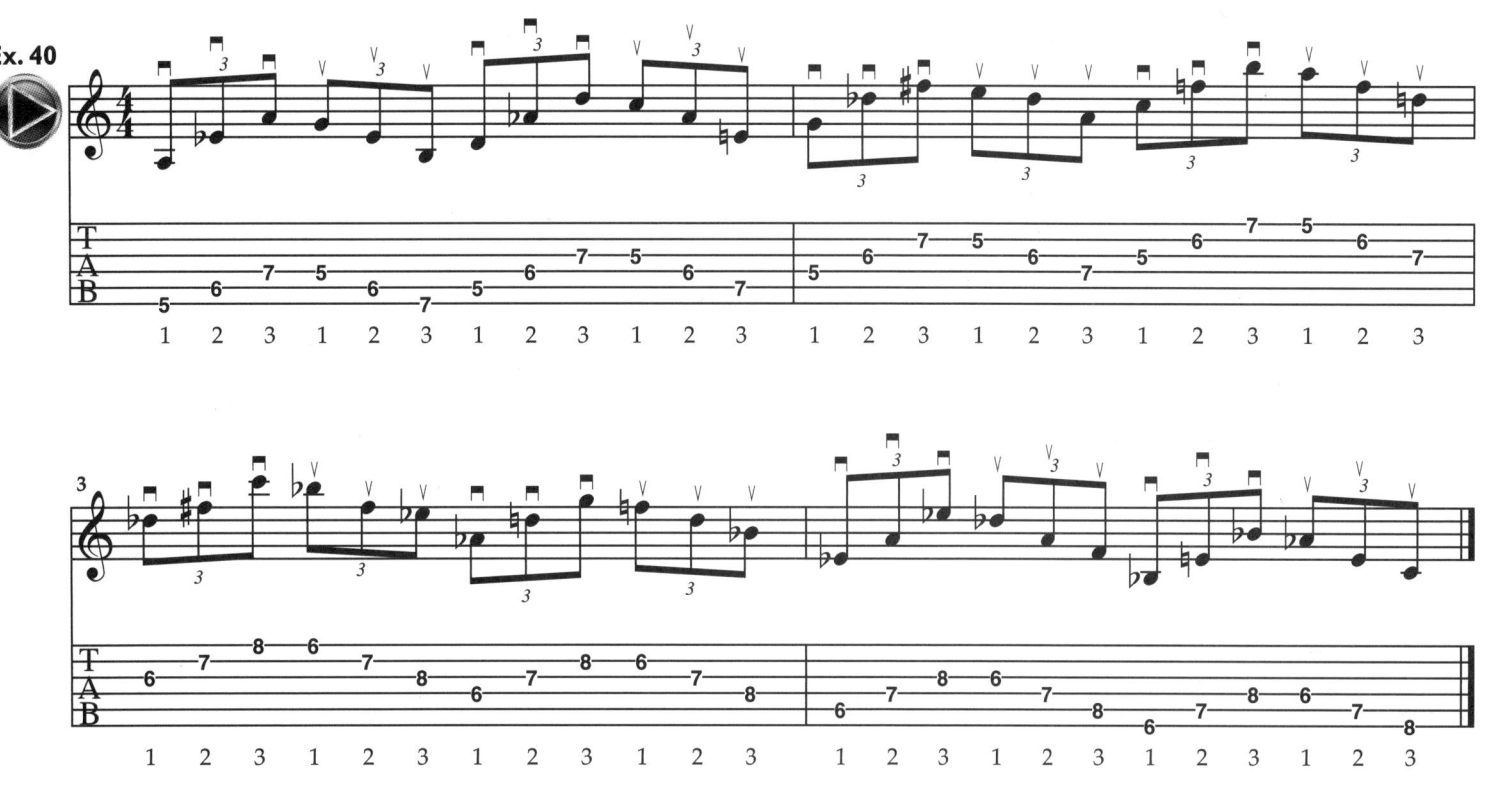

This next exercise uses all four fingers of your fretting hand. Play it slowly and with a clean sound.

Ex. 41

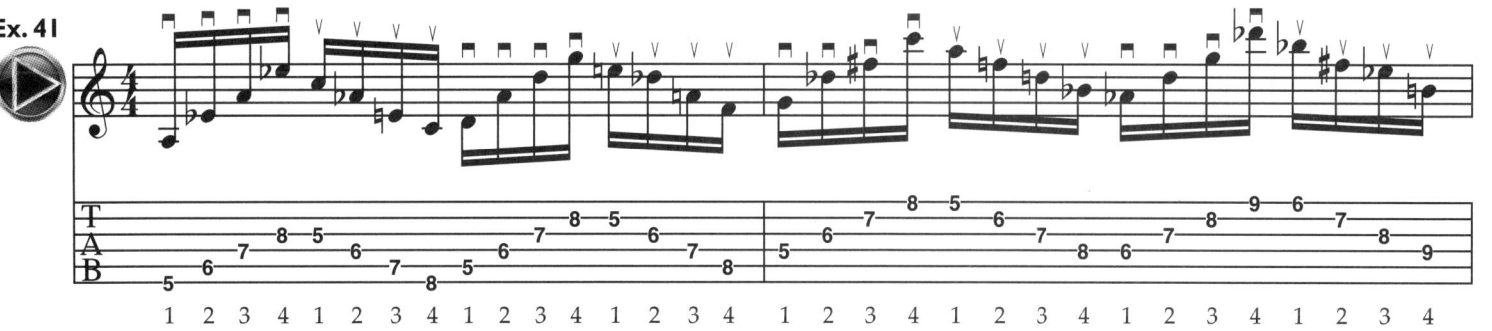

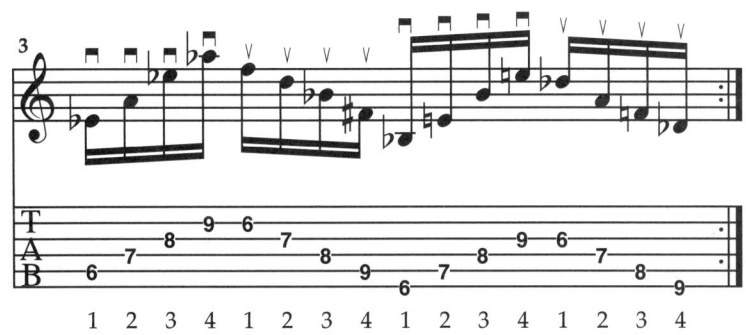

SHREDDING GUITAR WORKOUT

Two-String Sweeping

Two-string sweeping is an interesting and intense approach to playing several different ideas, not just simple arpeggio patterns. Let's start by playing different intervals on adjacent strings. Strive for a clean and even sound, and pay close attention to the correct notes and intervals.

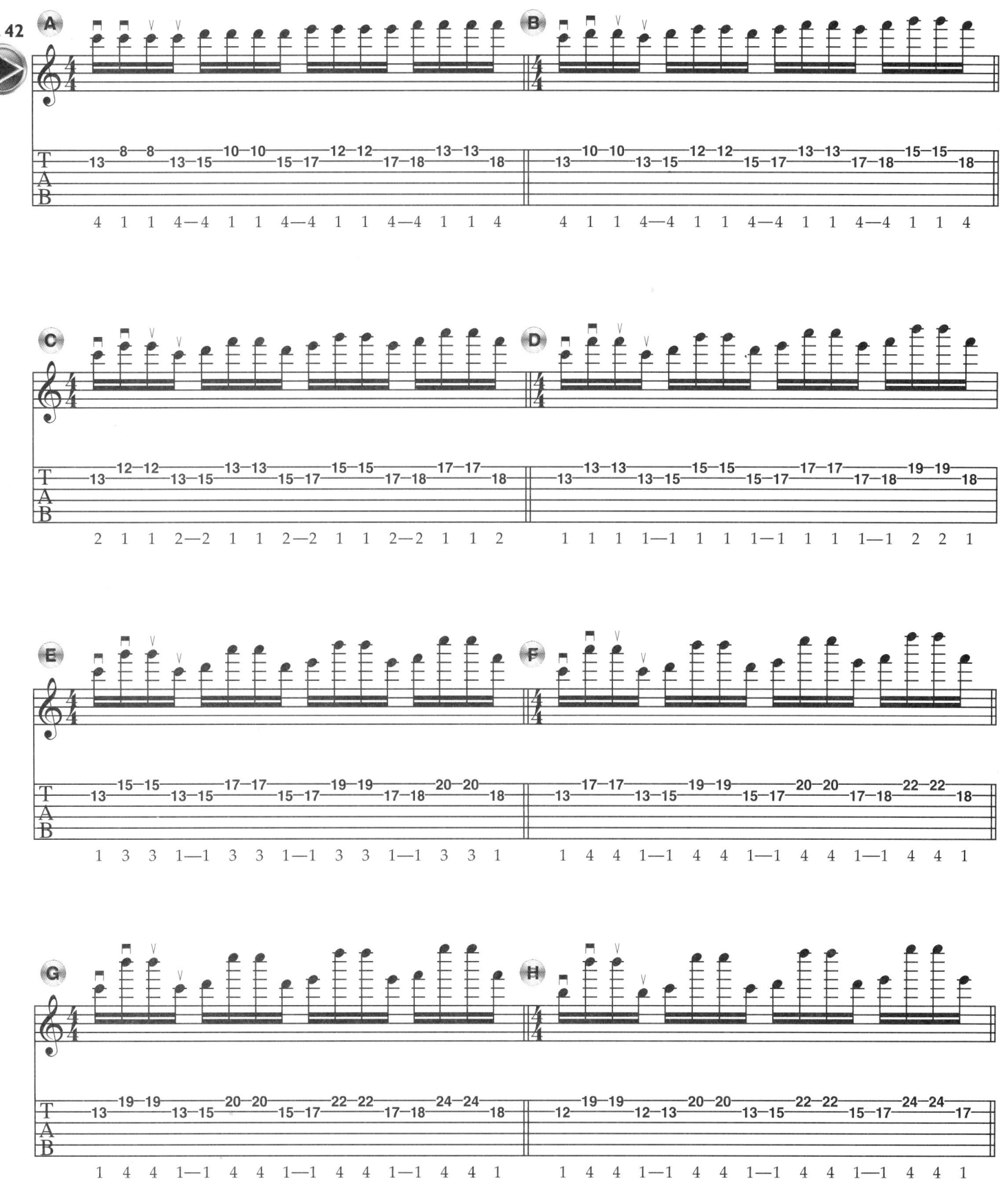

Try to practice all the different intervals on all adjacent strings and in all 12 keys.

The next exercise demonstrates how to play a *pedal-tone* idea using sweeping. A pedal tone is a repeated note (or phrase) played against an ascending or descending scale movement. The following example includes all possible diatonic intervals in the key of C Major.

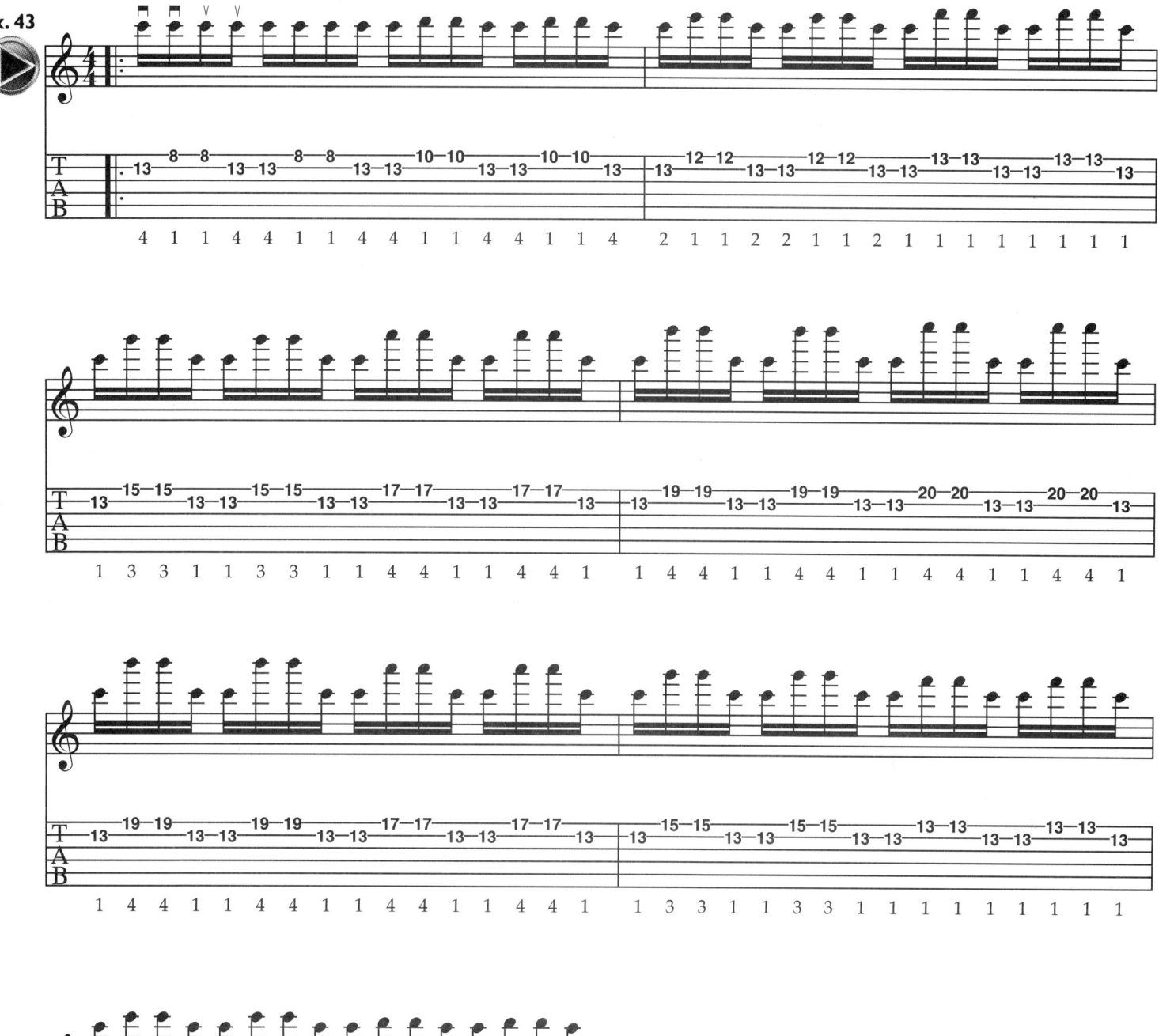

The next example utilizes chromaticism.

Ex. 44

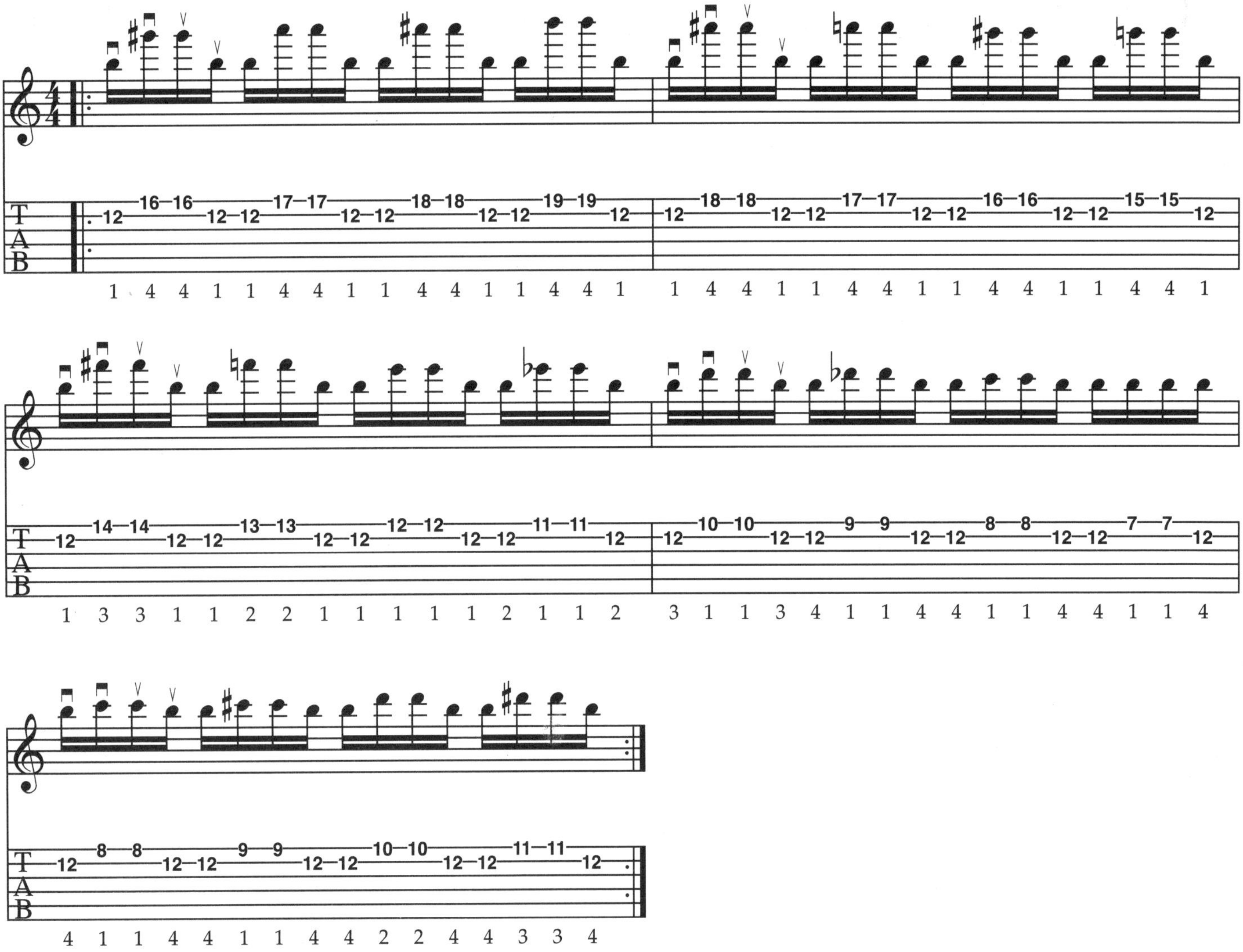

[Musical notation and tablature]

Try to practice these ideas on all adjacent strings and keys. In certain lower positions, this can be quite challenging due to the stretching required. Remember to practice slowly and patiently, and gradually increase your range and stretching abilities. Stop right away if you experience any pain or discomfort.

The next step is to play the different intervals across the strings. Pay close attention to your picking direction, and strive for a clean and even sound. Try the first measure below, then try the whole example on the next page.

Ex. 45

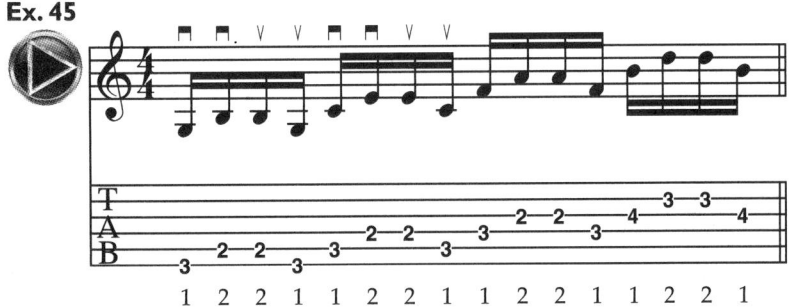

60 — Shredding Guitar Workout

Ex. 46

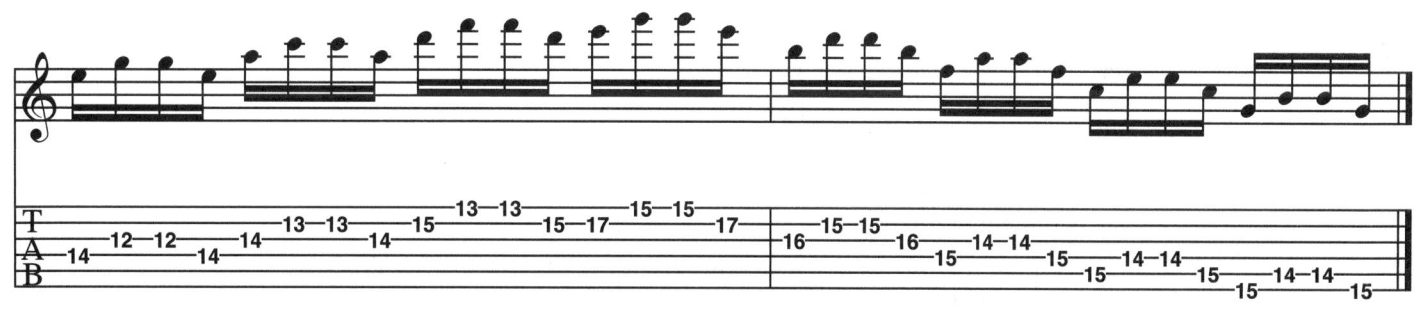

SHREDDING GUITAR WORKOUT — 61

Another great way to work on your sweep picking and fretboard knowledge is to combine different intervals with the basic underlying chords or harmony. This next example outlines a simple ascending chord progression in G Major.

Ex. 47

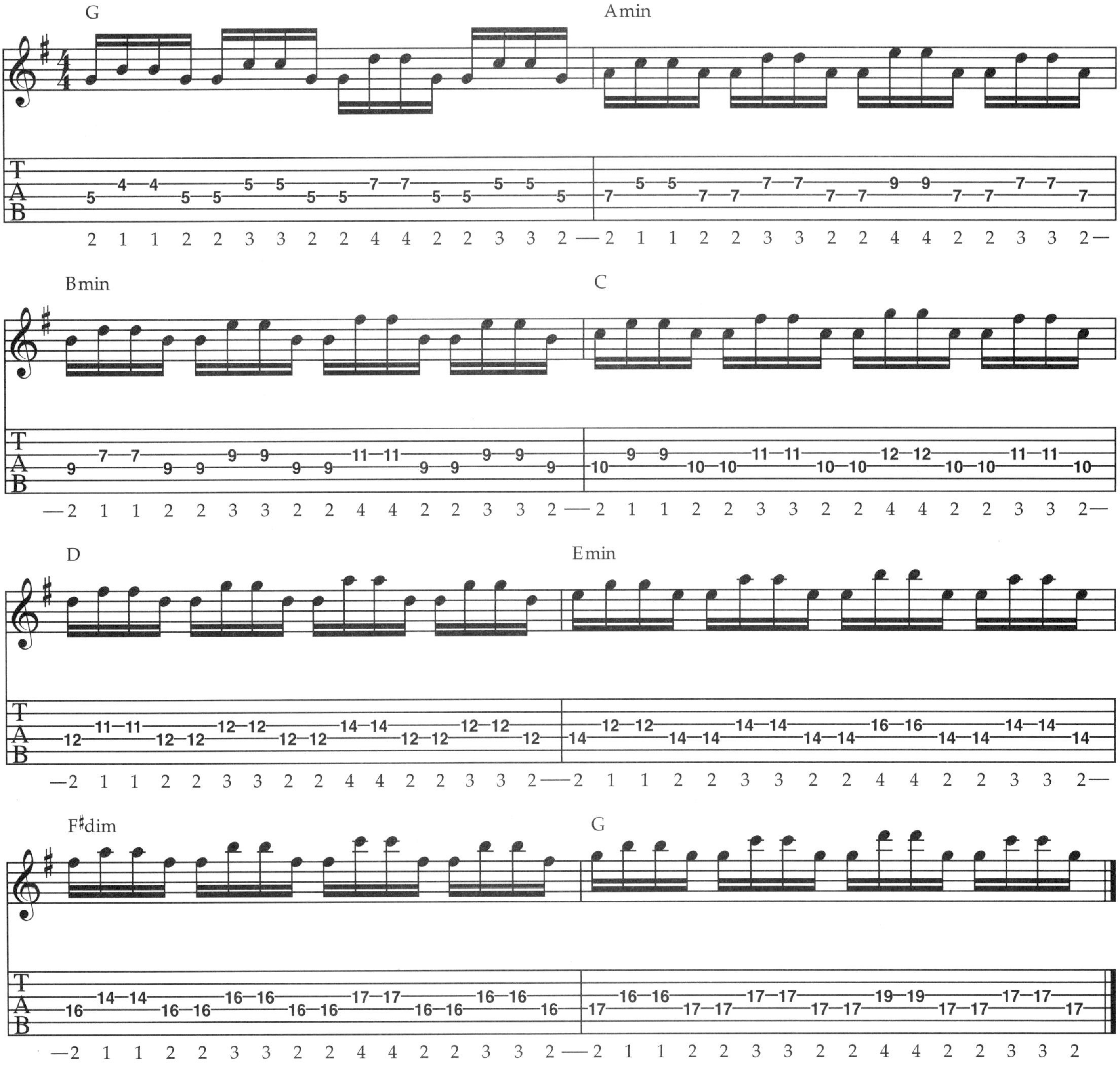

Now that you have experimented with this technique and its various possibilities, let's shift gears and focus on arpeggios. The diagrams below are the basic triads you can find in any key or within any scale.

Major

Minor

Diminished

Augmented

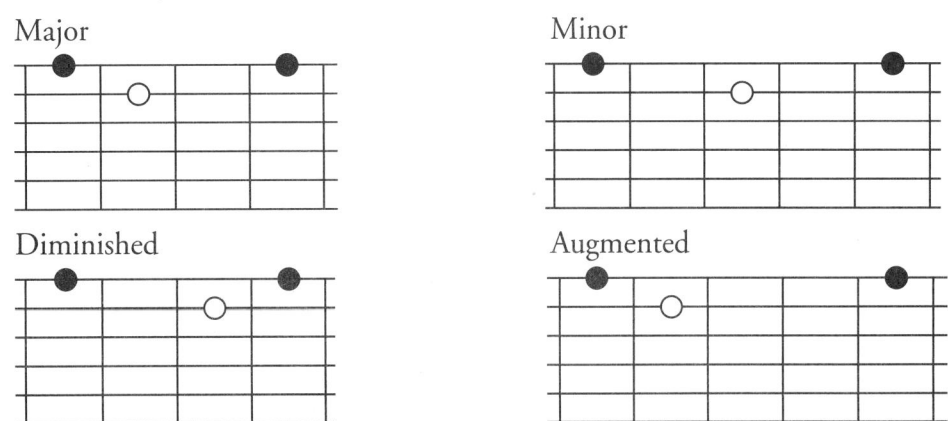

The triad shapes on the previous page can be played on all string sets and only require a slight adjustment when played on the 2nd and 3rd strings.

The next example features sweep patterns and ideas using two-string arpeggios.

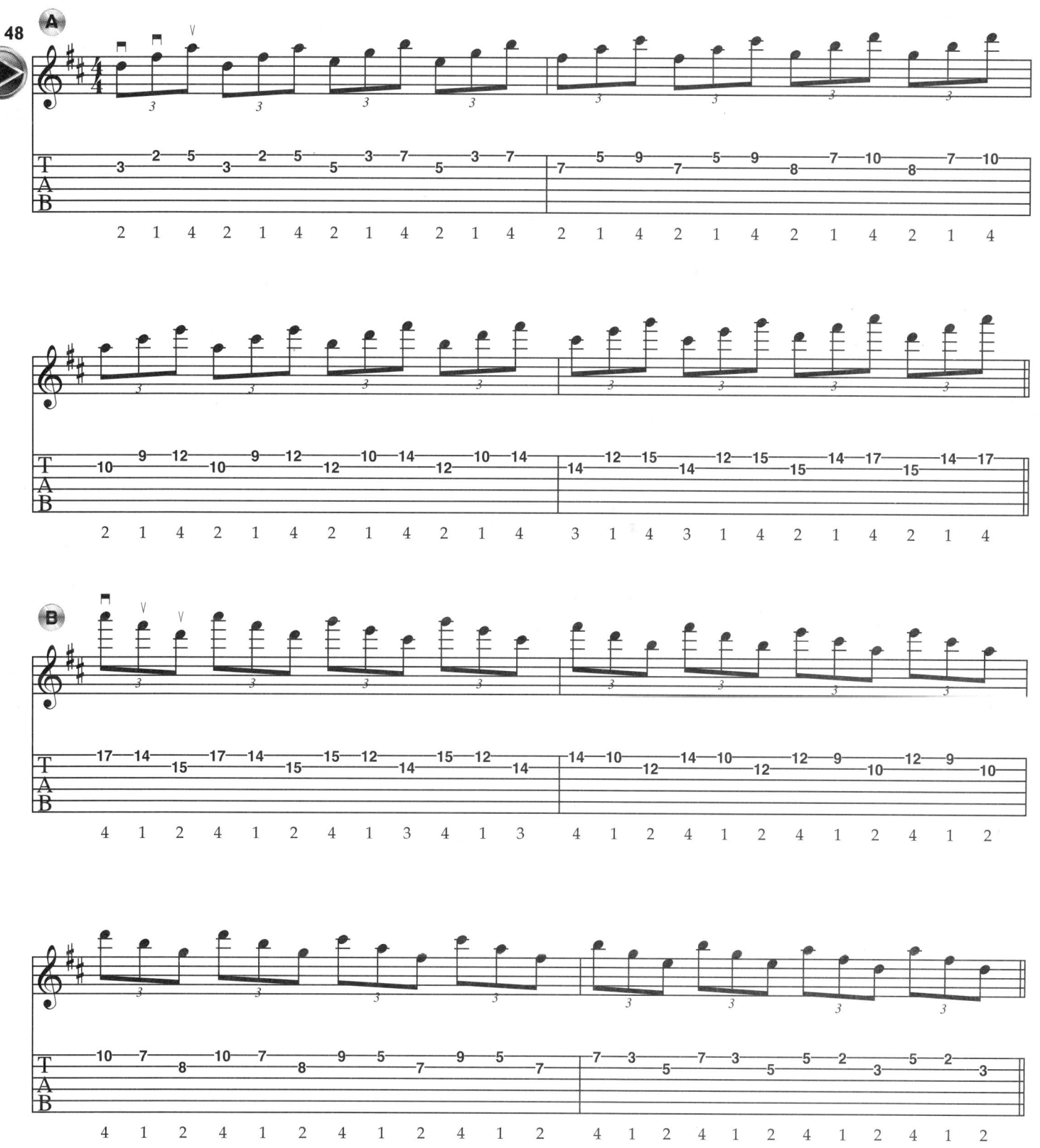

Example 49 shows a sixteenth-note rhythmic approach.

Ex. 49

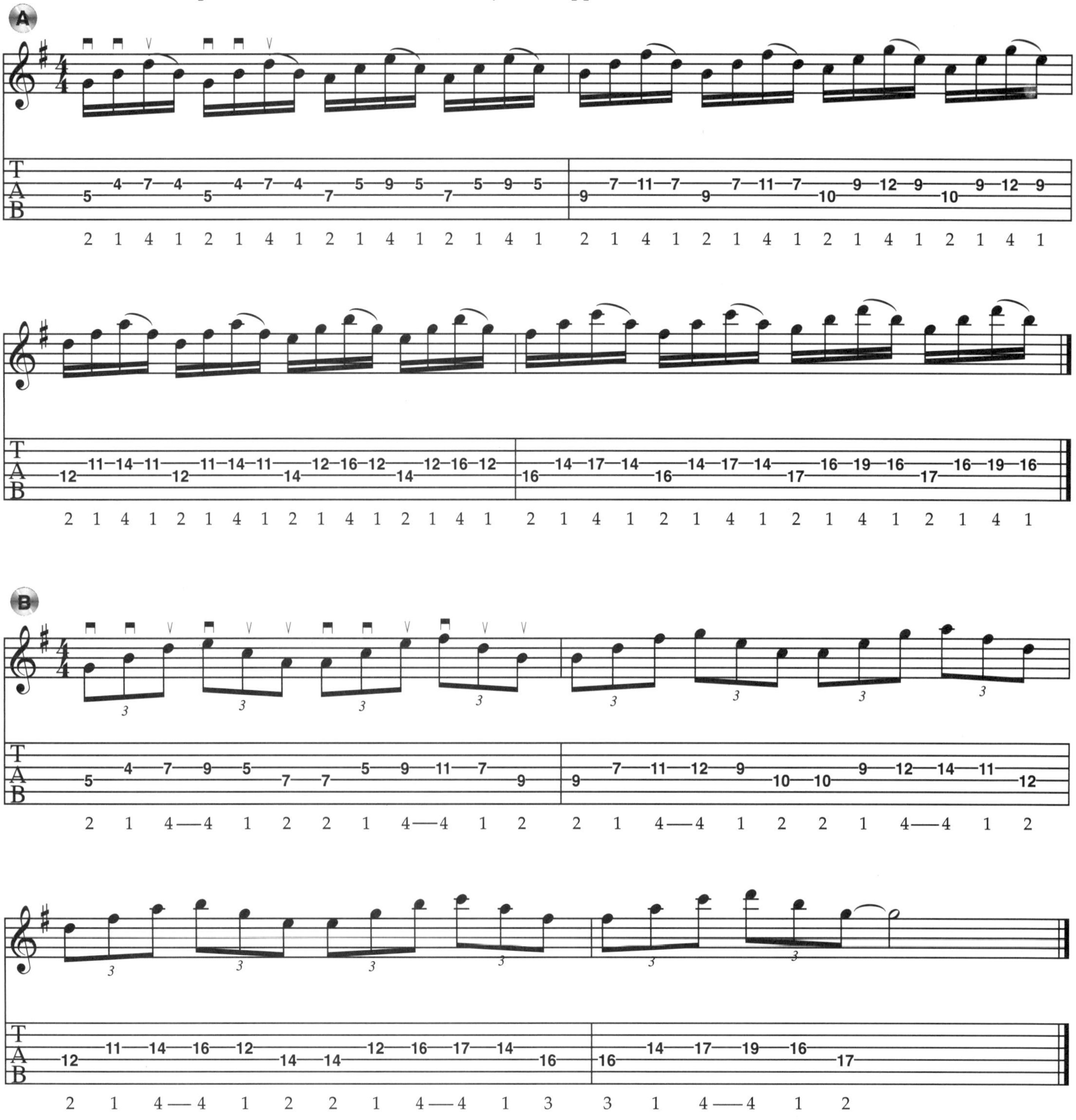

Here's another interesting variation featuring diatonic triads.

Ex. 50

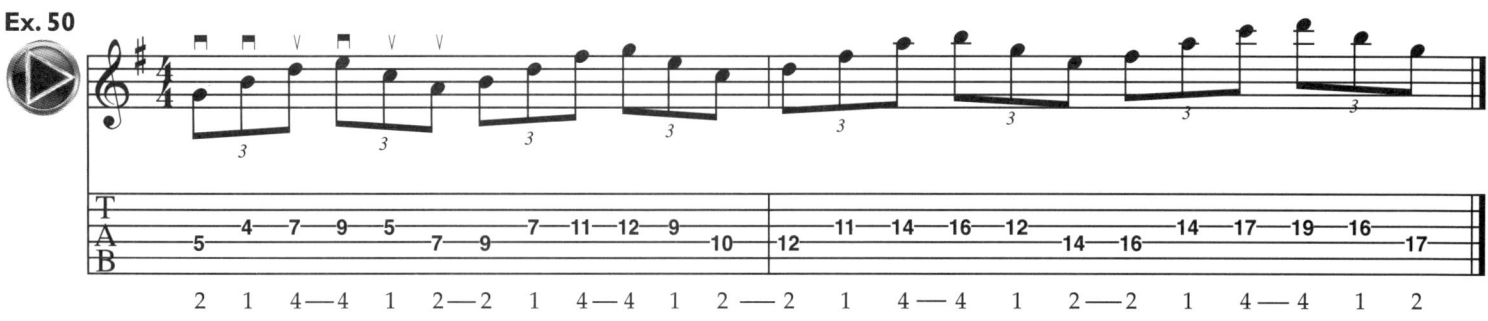

To freely use the sweeping technique in your improvisation, it's crucial to learn the diatonic triads across the fretboard leaping in 4th intervals, as demonstrated in the next example in the key of C Major.

Ex. 51

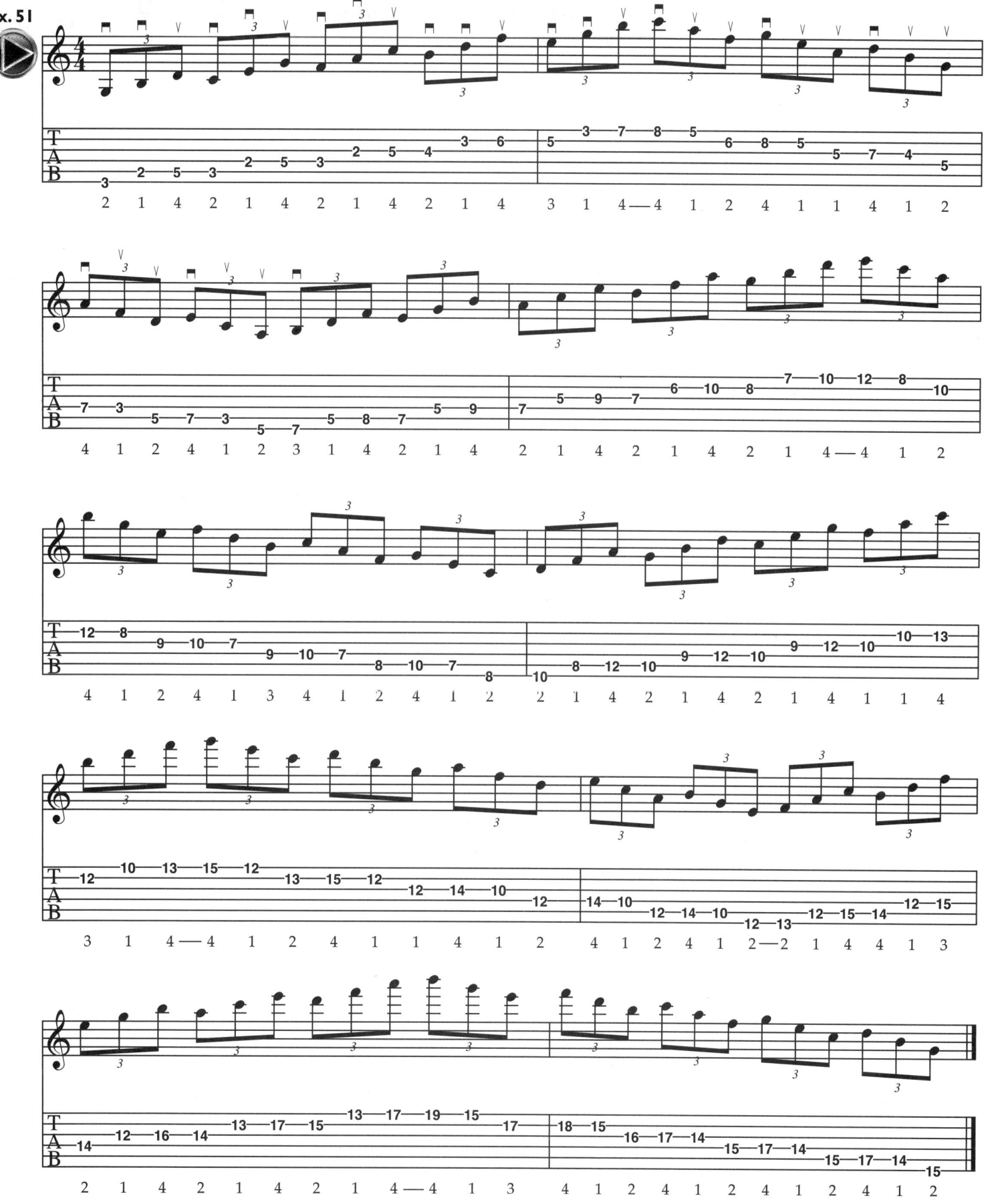

Shredding Guitar Workout

You can also play the ideas covered on the previous pages with different inversions of the triads. The next example shows C, Cmin, Cdim, and Caug in root position with all their inversions. Practice these arpeggios on all string sets and in different keys.

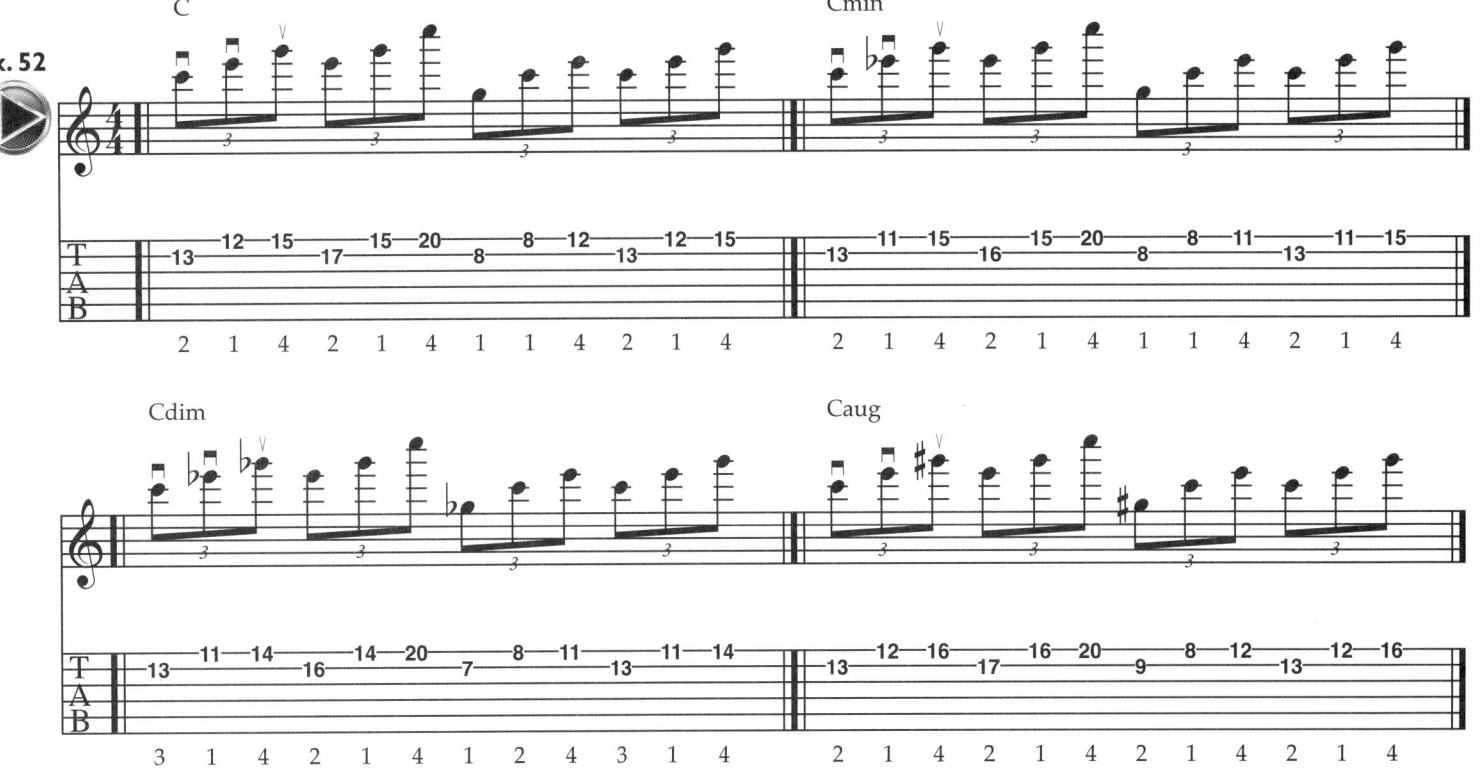

Three-String Sweeping

Now that you have mastered the two-string sweeping technique, let's move on to three-string sweeping. It is essential to learn the basic triad shapes in all inversions and on all string sets. All other arpeggio shapes are derived from these basic shapes, and once you have learned them, it's easy to learn the more extended shapes and develop your own as well.

The best way to work on technique and fretboard knowledge is to combine them in your practice routine. To do this, practice your arpeggios in a different key every day. The example below shows the basic picking pattern for a three-string sweep, using a C Major triad in root position.

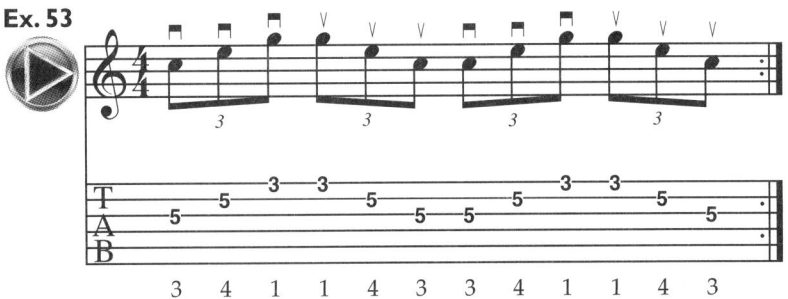

Shredding Guitar Workout

The next example features a simple three-string sweeping idea, harmonizing the key of C Major. Strive for an even sound.

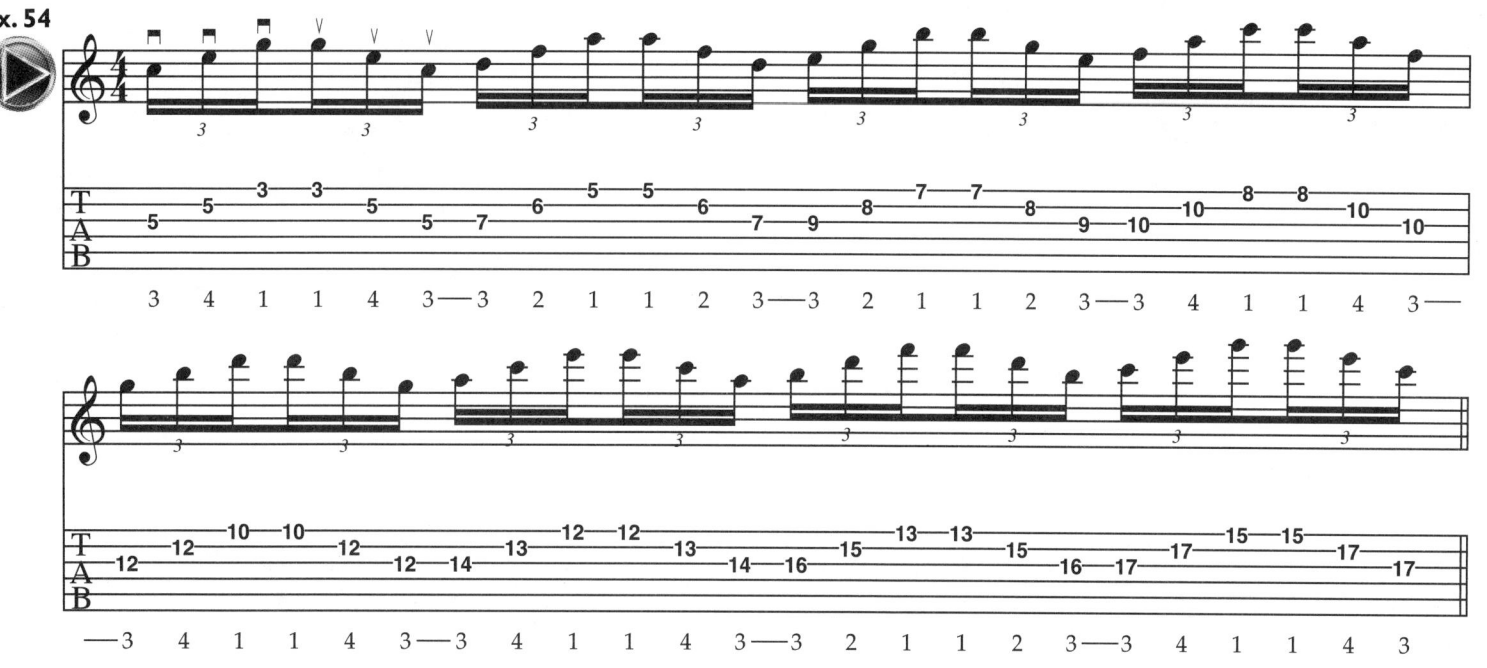

Extend your practice to all possible three-string combinations, using triads in root position or inversions. Practice slowly and make sure all notes are clear and audible.

Try this variation:

You can also extend your practice by adding *secondary dominants* (a dominant chord approaching a chord other than the I from a fifth above or fourth below) to the diatonic arpeggio progression. Try this example slowly and practice it on all strings.

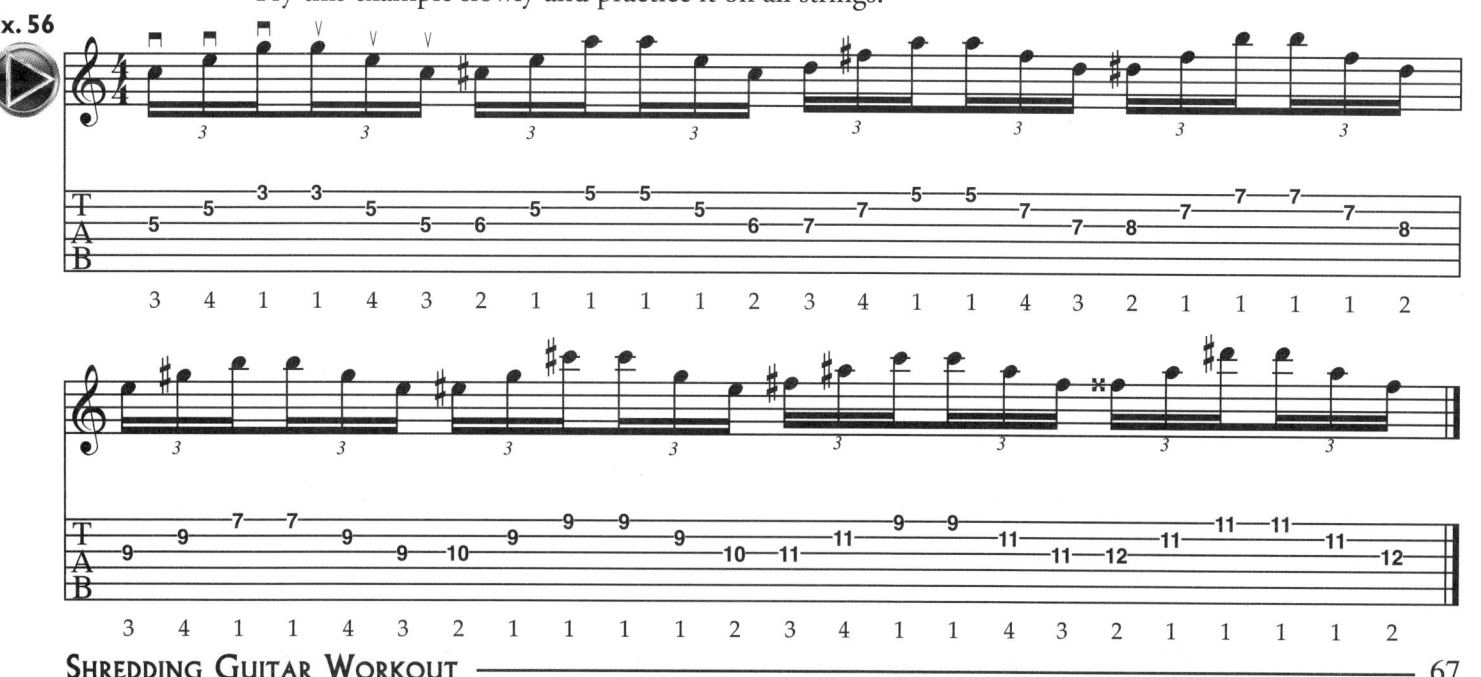

The next example demonstrates the triads in the key of C Major played across the fretboard, with the root notes ascending in 4ths. This is the ultimate sweeping and triad knowledge workout! Don't forget to also practice this in all 12 keys.

Ex. 57

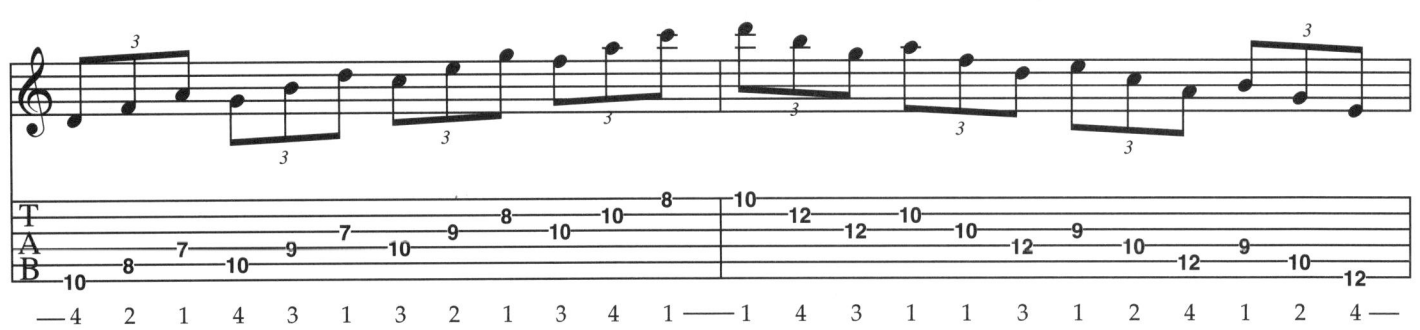
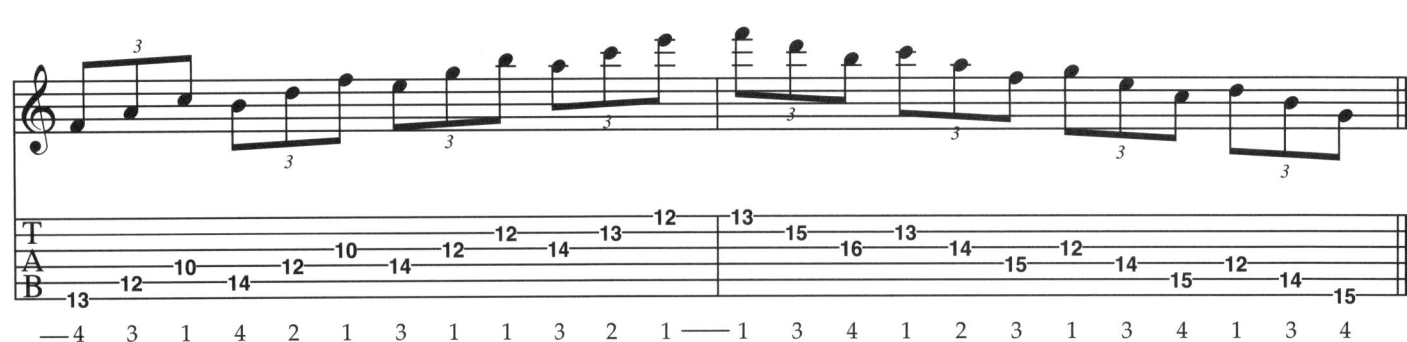

Five-String Sweeping

The next step is to combine all of our triad patterns to form five-, six-, or even seven-string arpeggios. From there, you can then isolate or focus on separate string sections and combinations. The diagrams below show the complete five-string major, minor, diminished, and augmented triads.

Major Triad

Root Position

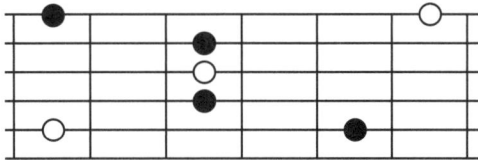

1st Inversion

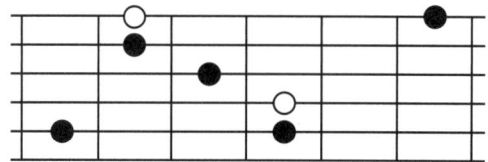

2nd Inversion

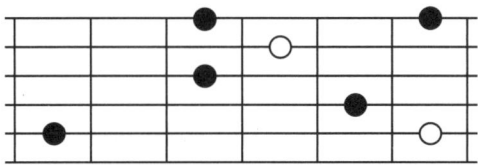

Minor Triad

Root Position

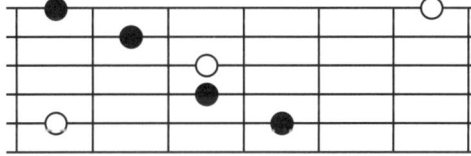

1st Inversion

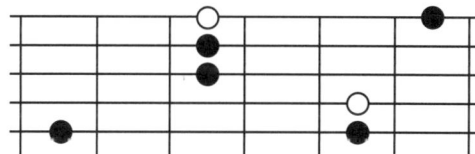

2nd Inversion

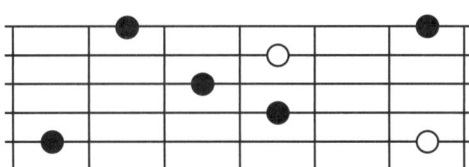

Diminished Triad

2nd Inversion

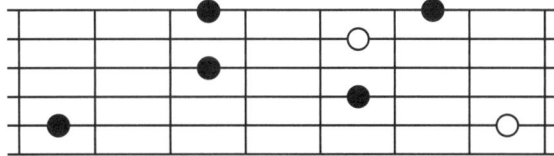

Augmented Triad

2nd Inversion

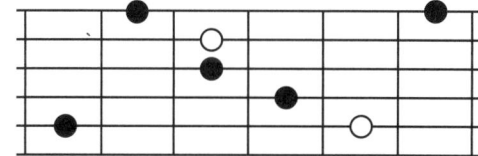

The diminished and augmented triads are shown only in 2nd inversion, because these shapes are easiest to execute with sweeping. However, you should try them in other inversions as well.

The following examples feature common three- and four-string arpeggio patterns. These patterns are derived from the larger 5-string arpeggio shapes. Practice them in different keys. Also, apply these basic patterns to diatonic progressions in various keys, and don't forget to include inversions.

Ex. 58

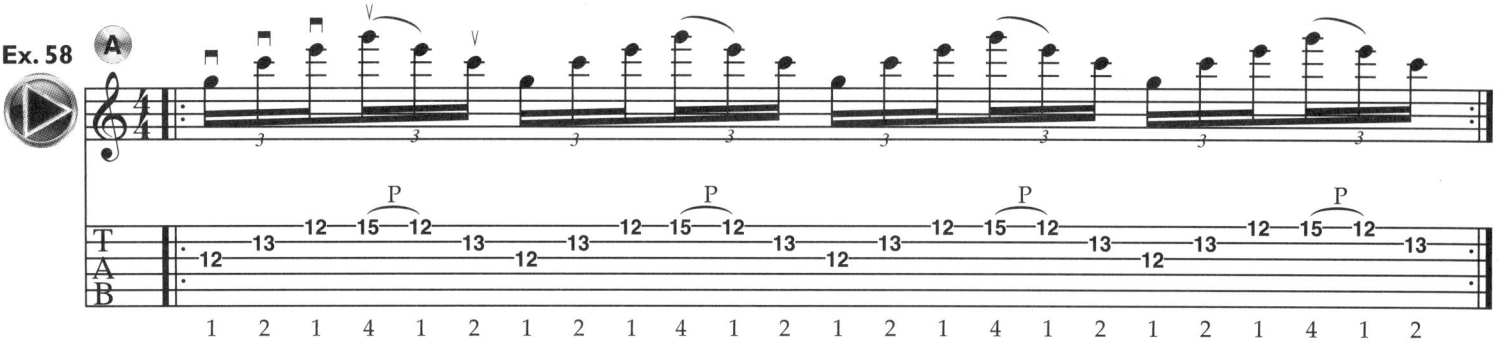

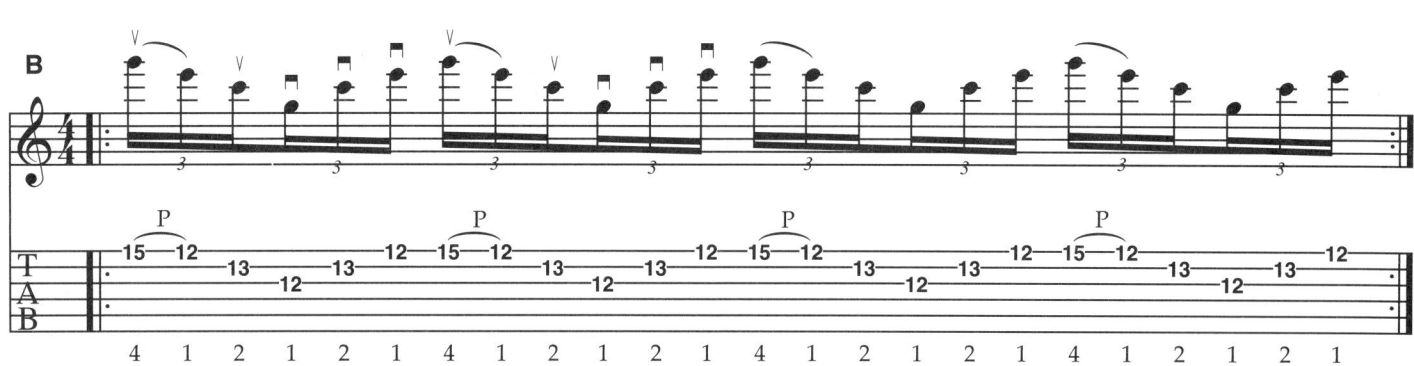

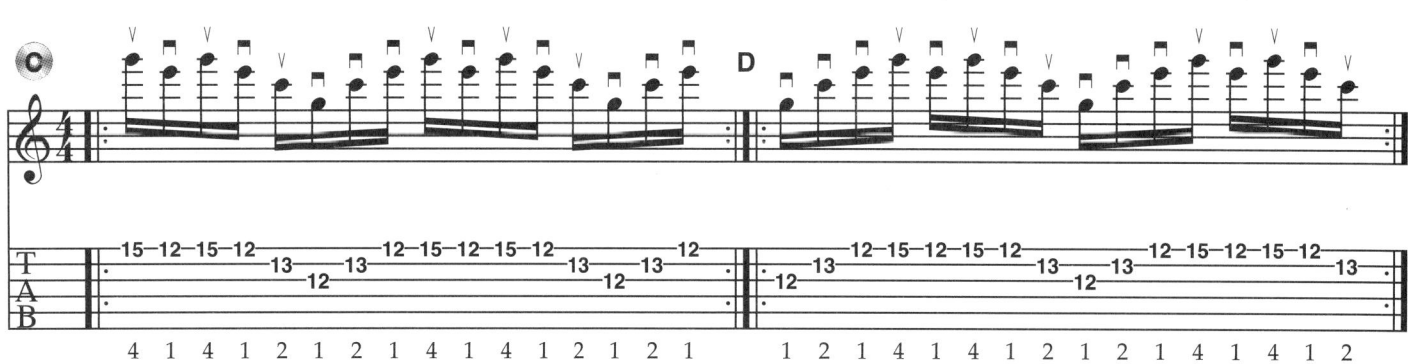

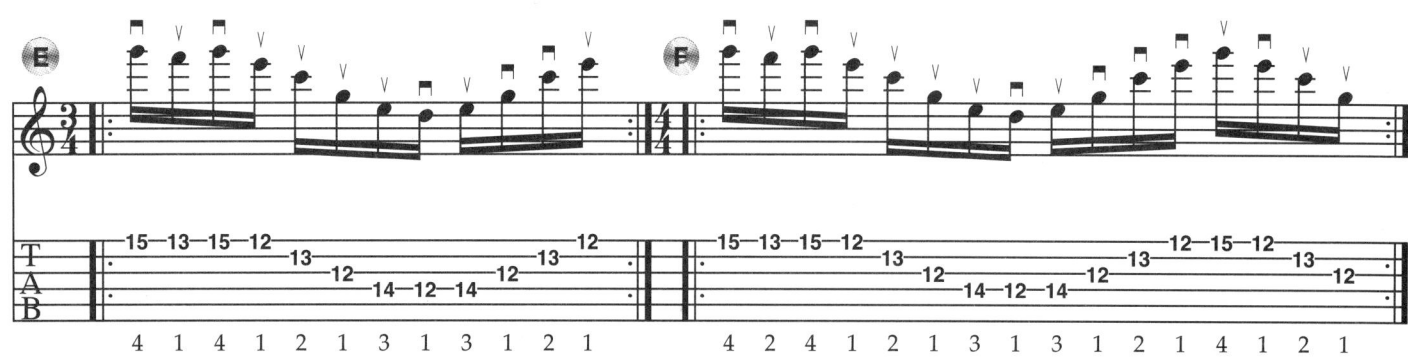

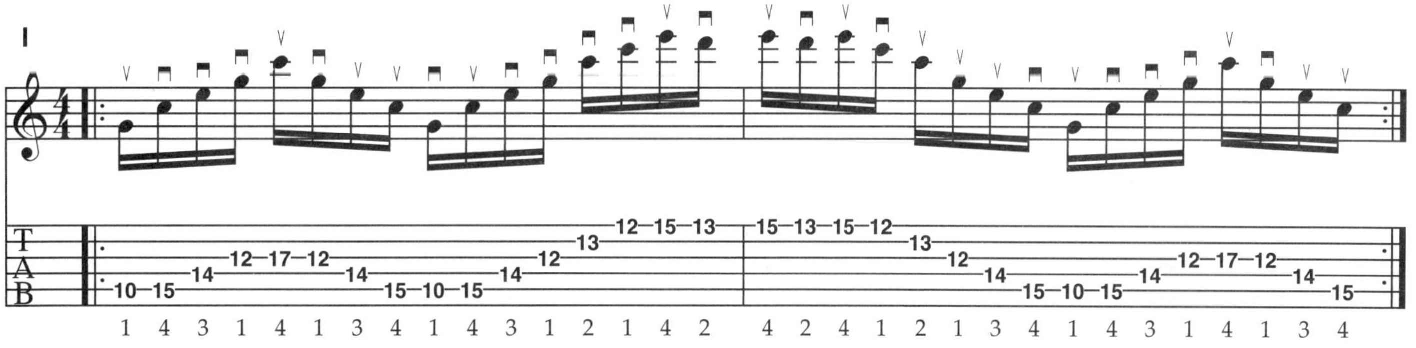

Below is another variation that adds secondary dominants to progress through a key.

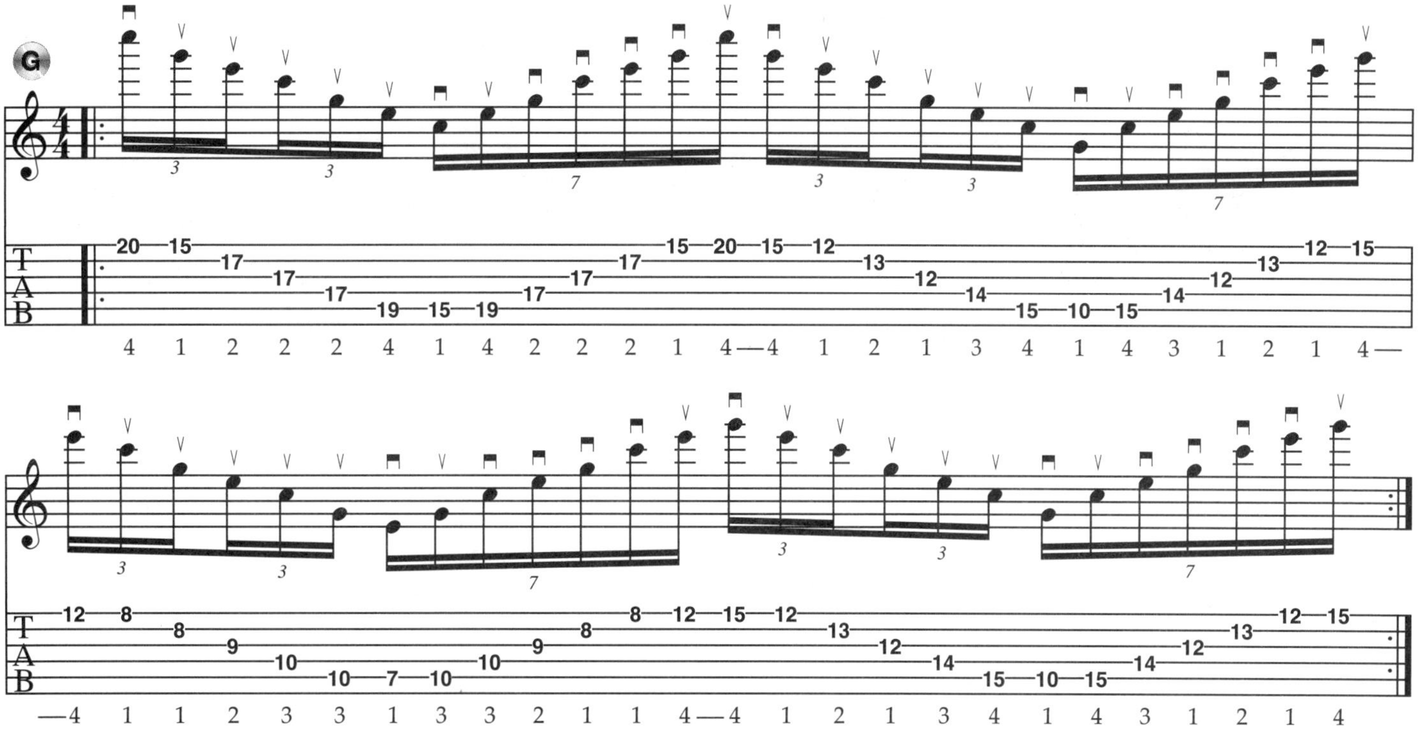

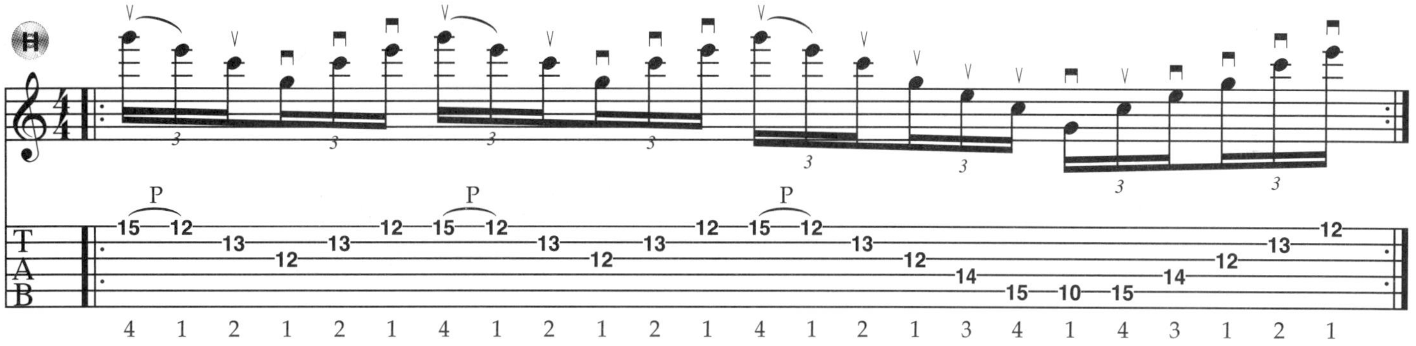

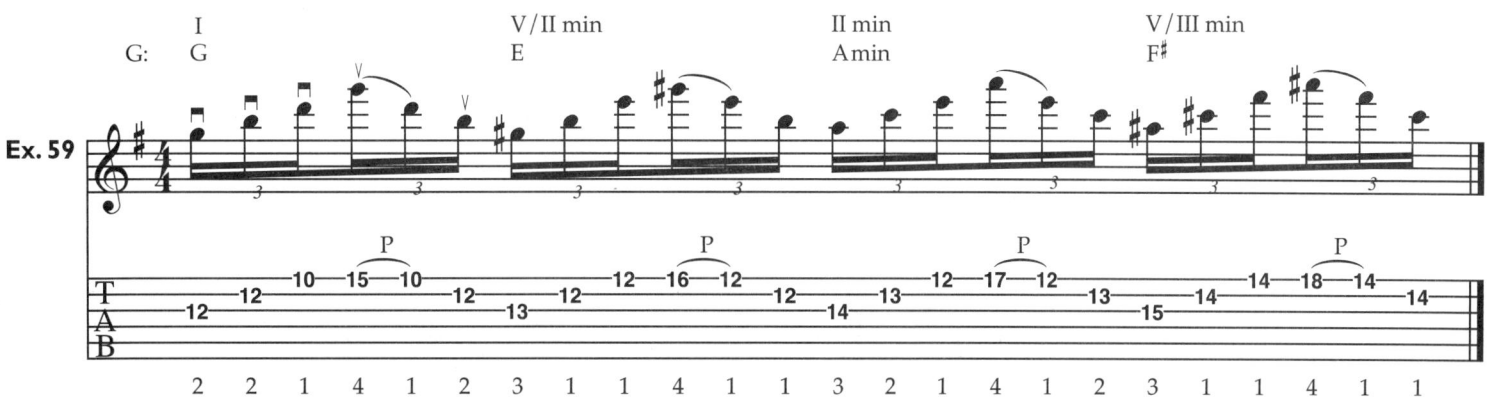

Shredding Guitar Workout

You can create long, cascading arpeggio sequences by combining smaller and larger triad shapes.

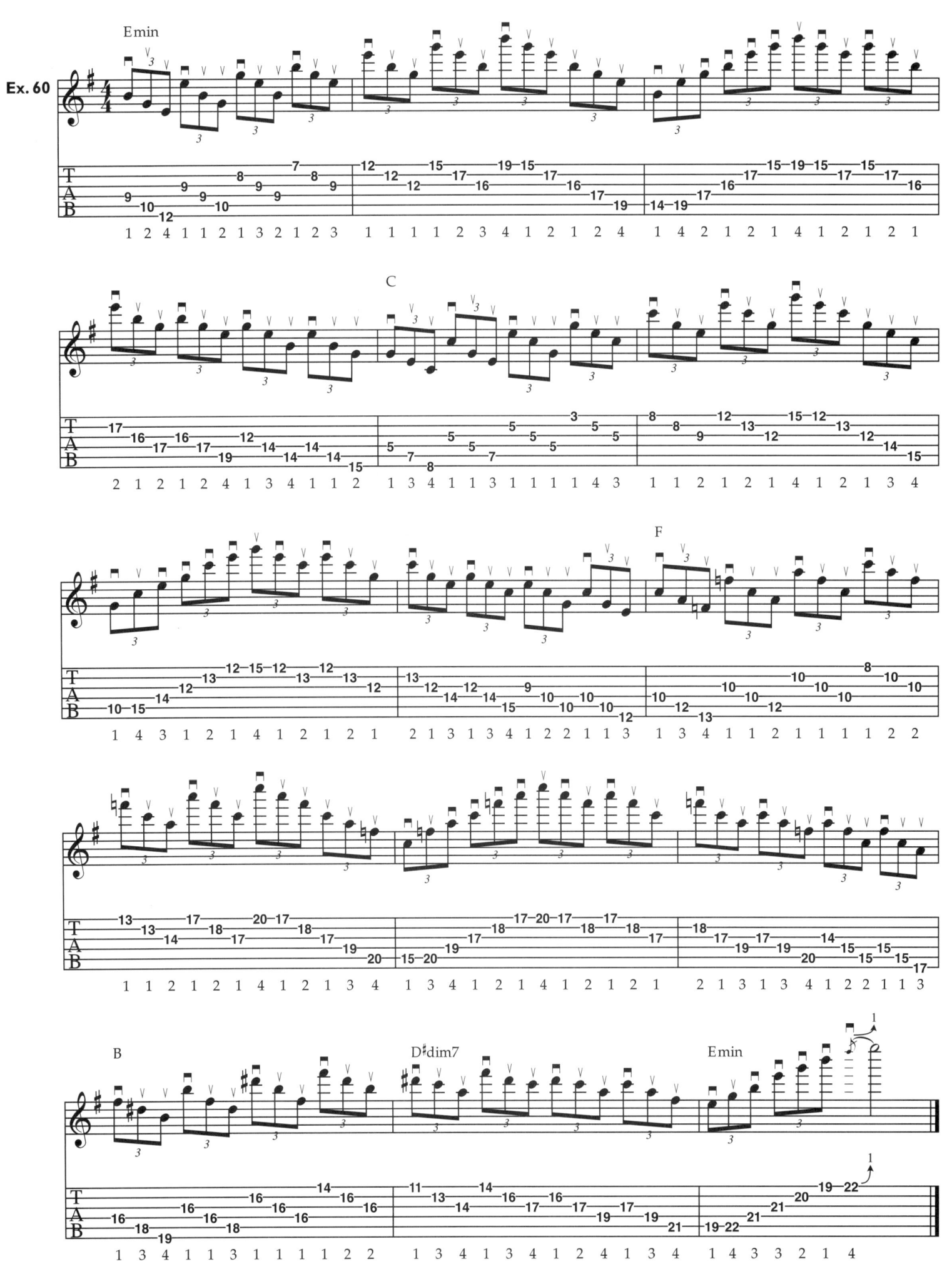

Try to develop your own patterns and ideas, applying your knowledge of theory.

Five-String 7th Arpeggios

Are you looking for more possibilities? Let's check out 7th-chord arpeggios, which are based on the basic triads but have one more 3rd stacked on top of the 5th. There are many different fingerings for these arpeggios but the most appropriate are shown below.

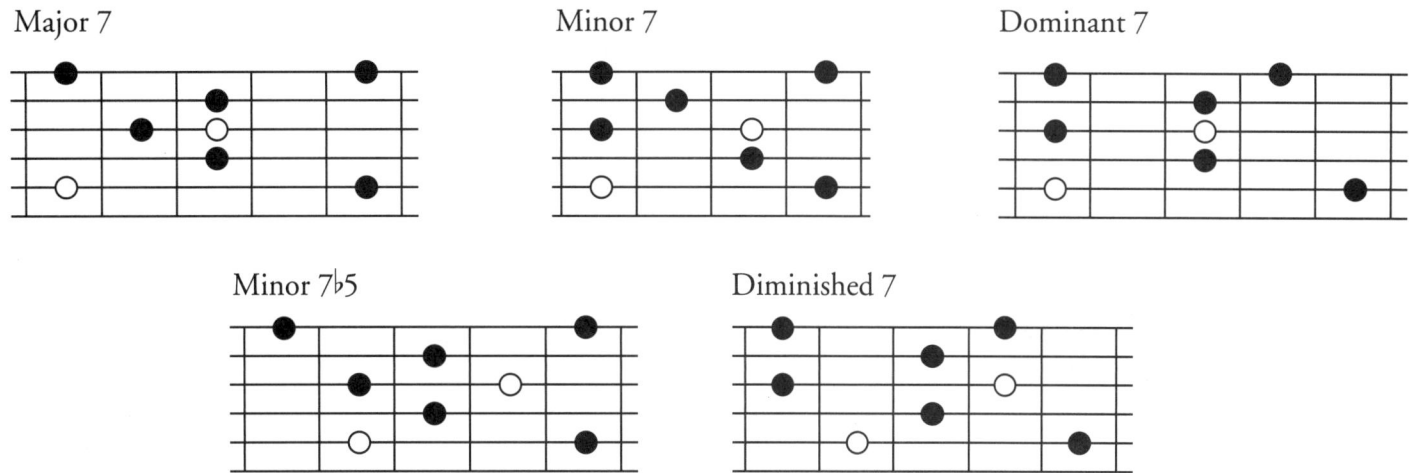

Play slowly through the shapes above and try to memorize them. The picking patterns for simple ascending or descending 7th-chord arpeggios are divided into two different octaves, one with the root on the 3rd string and one with the root on the 5th string. Apply these patterns to the different shapes, and play them slowly and accurately. Keep your metronome on hand to precisely dial in the tempo, as it is normal to rush when sweeping.

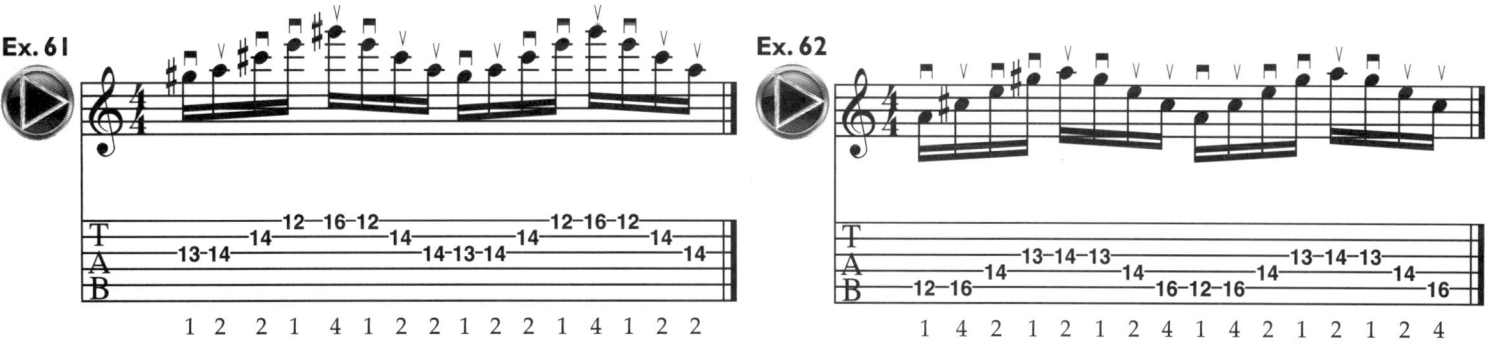

After learning all the shapes, try to harmonize a major or minor scale, like below.

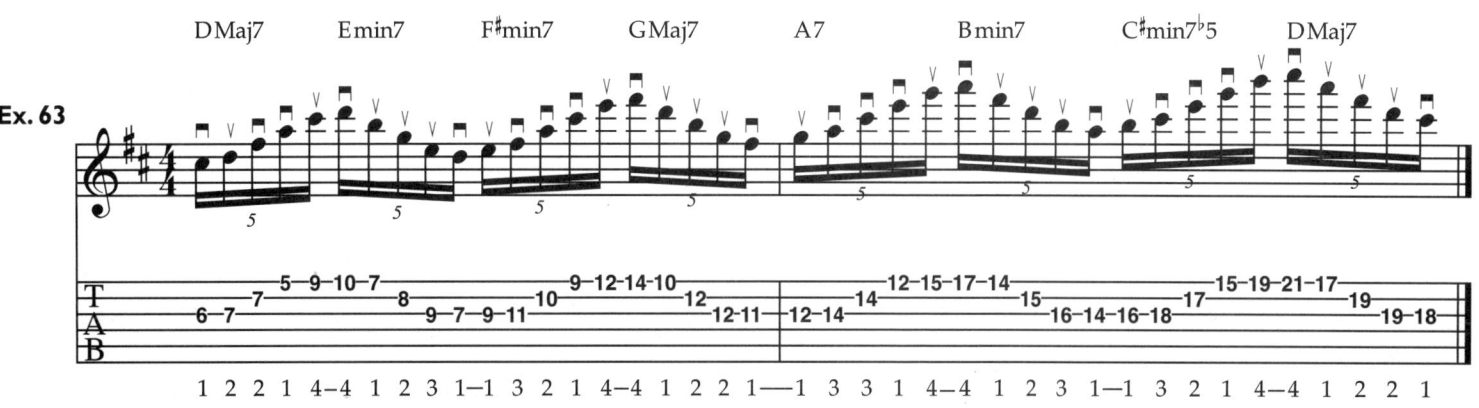

Shredding Guitar Workout

Now, let's combine the two octaves and create a simple ascending arpeggio sequence.

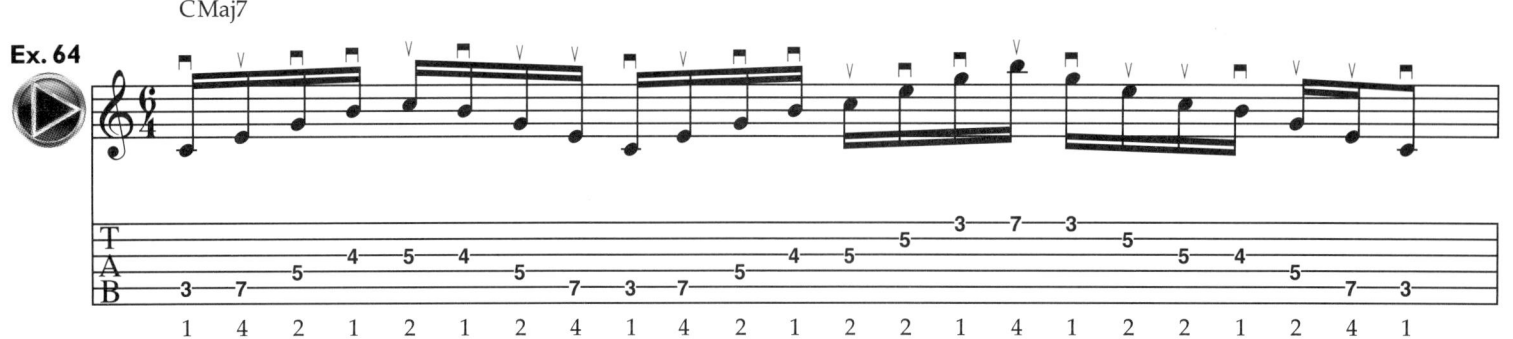

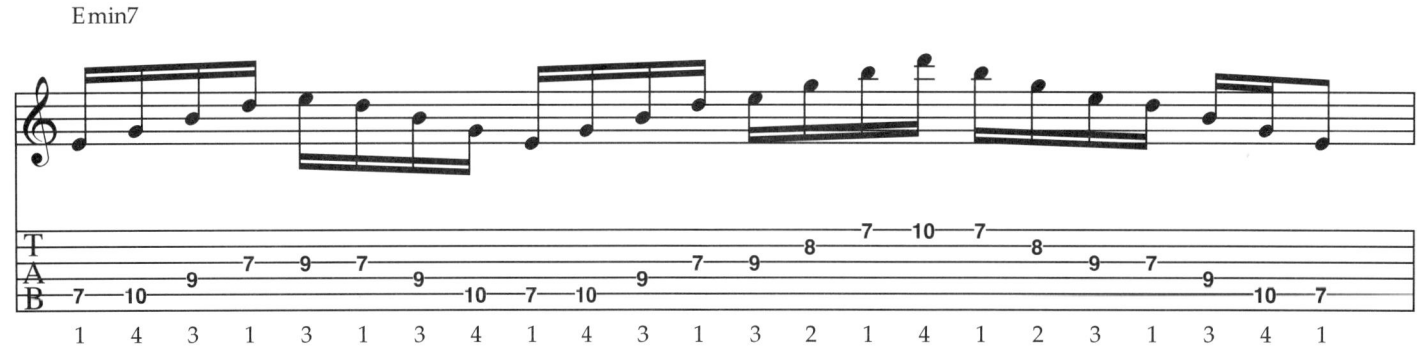

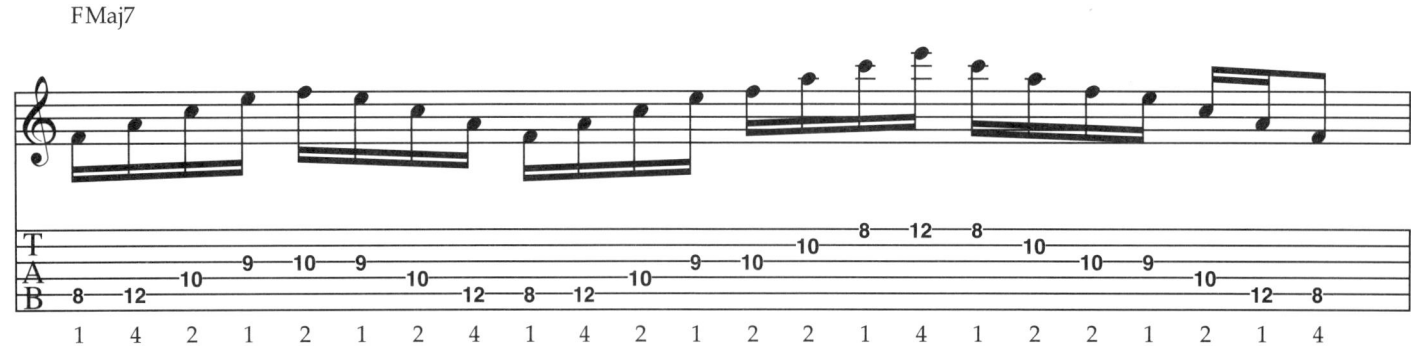

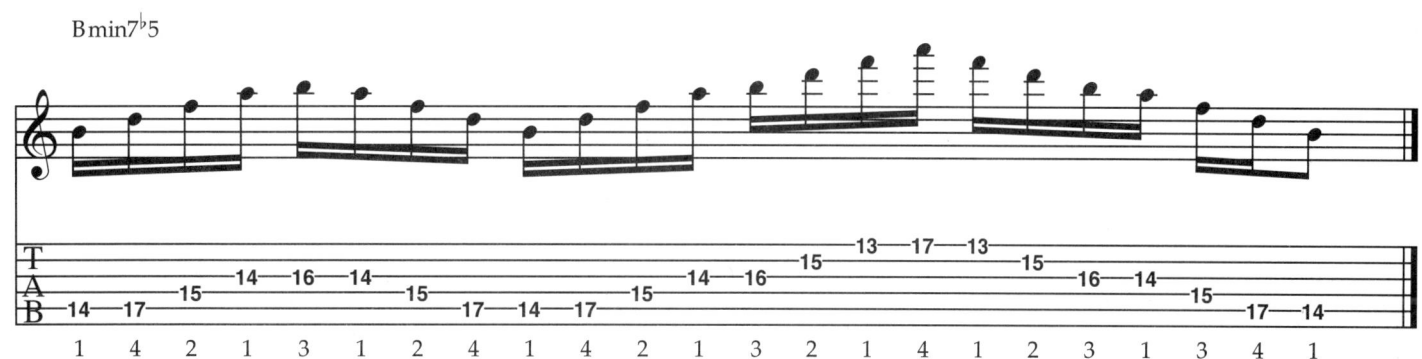

Try to experiment with developing different chord progressions, or simply arpeggiate the chord progression of a familiar song.

Arpeggio Shapes for the Seven-String Guitar

Let's take a look at extended-range arpeggios. If you are a seven-string guitar player, you have a lot of different options for playing scales and arpeggios. All of this, however, is still based on the same basic shapes. You can simply extend the range of the 7th arpeggios by adding the appropriate shape to the lower octave, on the 7th string.

Ex. 65

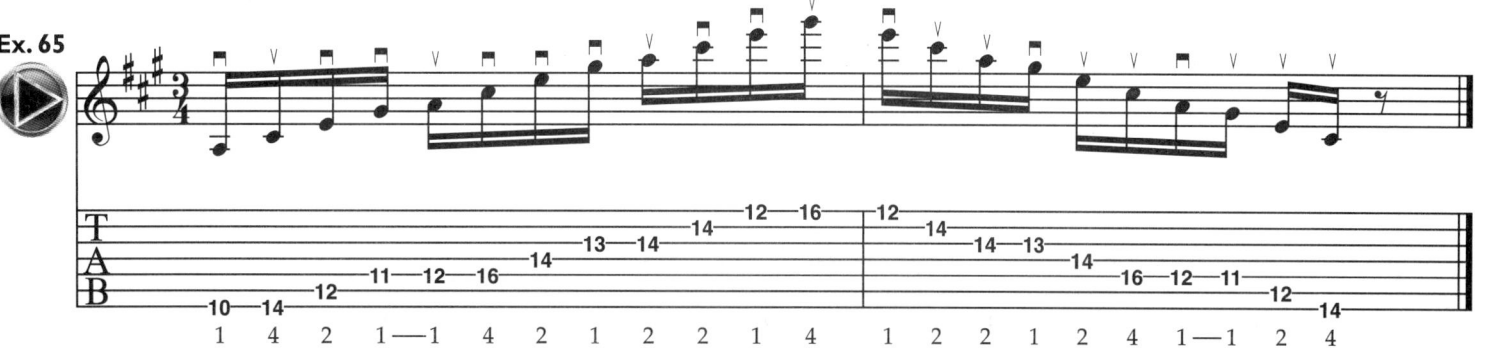

SHREDDING GUITAR WORKOUT — 75

Let's take a look at the basic triads and their inversions for the seven-string guitar.

Major Triad Arpeggio Shapes and Inversions

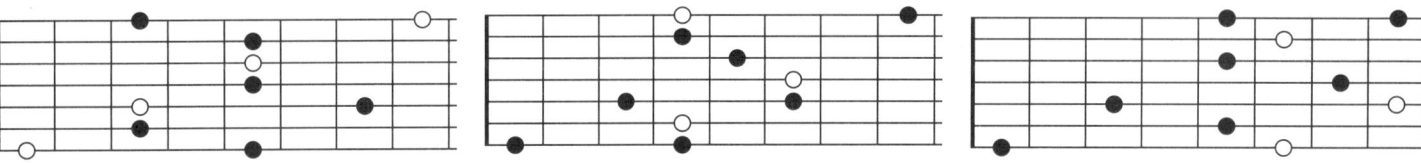

Minor Triad Arpeggio Shapes and Inversions

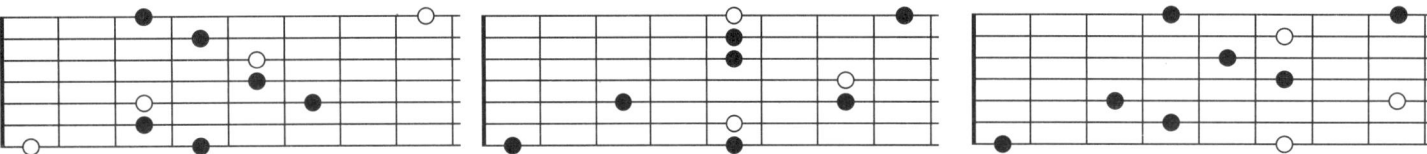

Diminished Arpeggio Shape

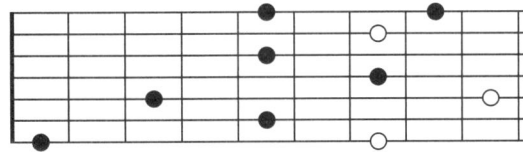

Memorize the shapes above and practice them with the patterns and ideas covered so far. Start out slowly, as it takes time to get used to the wide range of each arpeggio.

Ex. 66

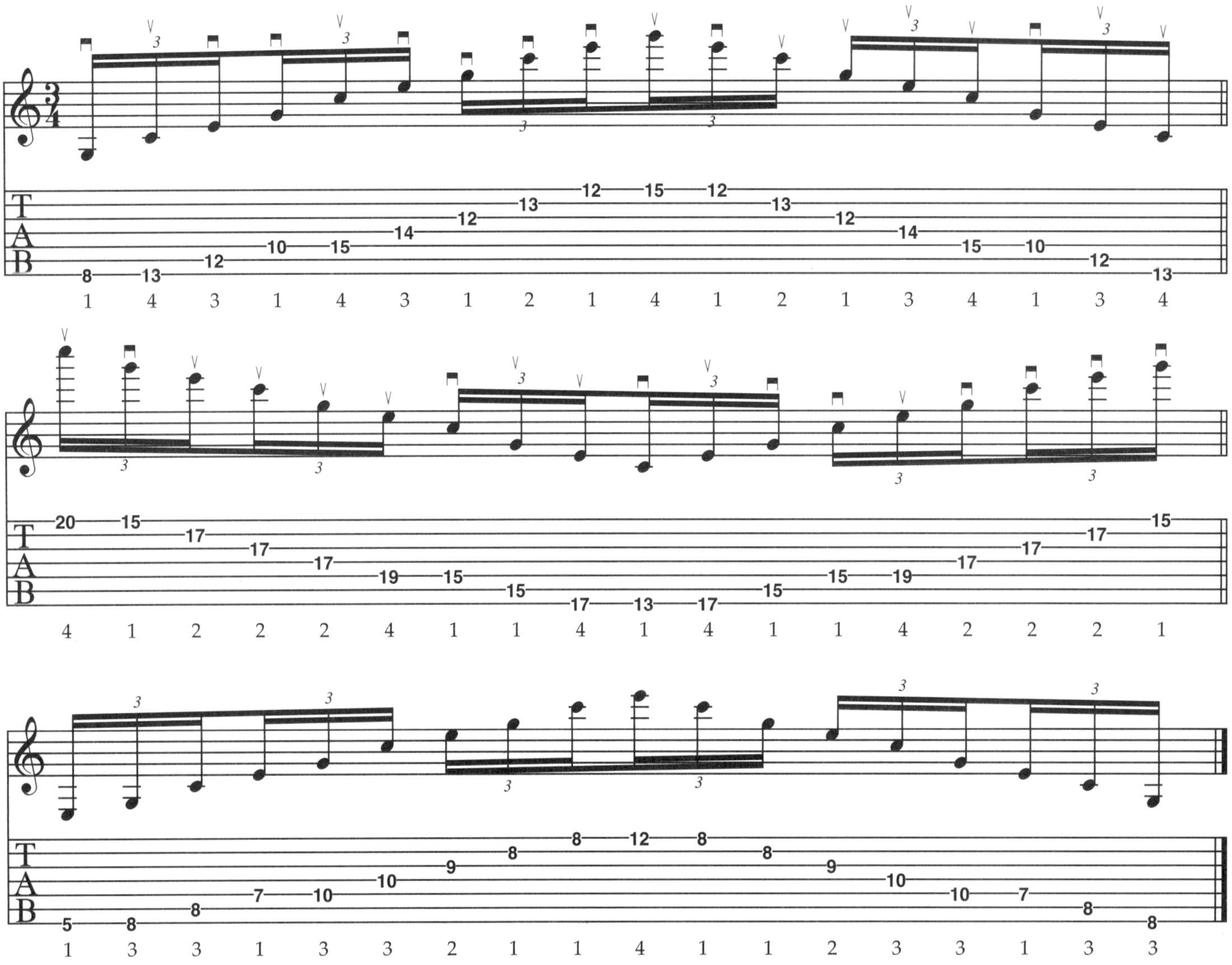

LEGATO TECHNIQUE

Legato means to play in a smooth and flowing manner, without separate attacks on each note. This technique utilizes hammer-ons, pull-offs, and slides to create a fluid sound without the *staccato* effect (short, abbreviated) produced by constant picking.

To execute effective legato passages, it's important to develop the right muscles in your fretting hand and learn precise finger placement on the strings so that you are producing clear and accurate tones.

The following chromatic exercises will help you develop good technique as well as warm up your hands. Try to relax and play the notes without too much pressure. If fretted too hard, the pitches will be slightly off and your hand will get tired quickly. Short practice intervals are very important in order to avoid muscle fatigue. Also, as always, use a metronome to monitor your progress and maintain good timing.

Move the following exercises to other strings and also play them in different positions.

Legato Warm-Ups

The following exercises take a similar idea and move it across the fretboard. At first, make sure you play these slowly, accurately, and with a steady pace. You can move the starting point to any position you like.

Remember, don't use too much force when fretting, as the notes will go out of pitch. You may also try to play these exercises without any initial pick strokes, relying solely on the correct and perfect placement of your fingers to sound the notes.

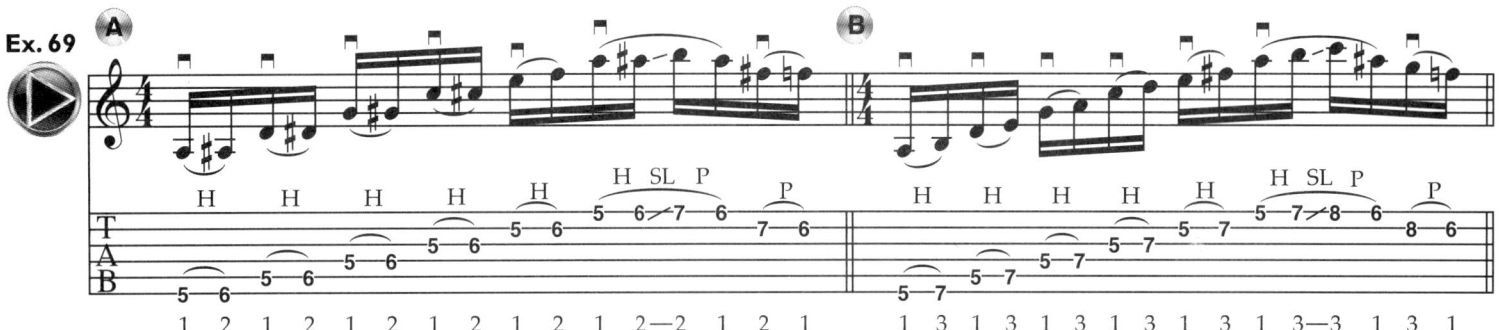

One- and Two-String Legato Patterns

Playing patterns and ideas based on the legato technique opens up a whole new way of phrasing and creating sounds on the guitar. The following melodic one- and two-string exercises will help you build a good vocabulary. When practicing these fragments, use a metronome and make sure you understand the implied rhythm of each phrase. Move the patterns up and down on all strings and make the necessary diatonic adjustments to stay in the keys you are working in.

Our first group of exercises consists of triplet patterns (and don't forget, you can play these as sextuplet rhythms, too).

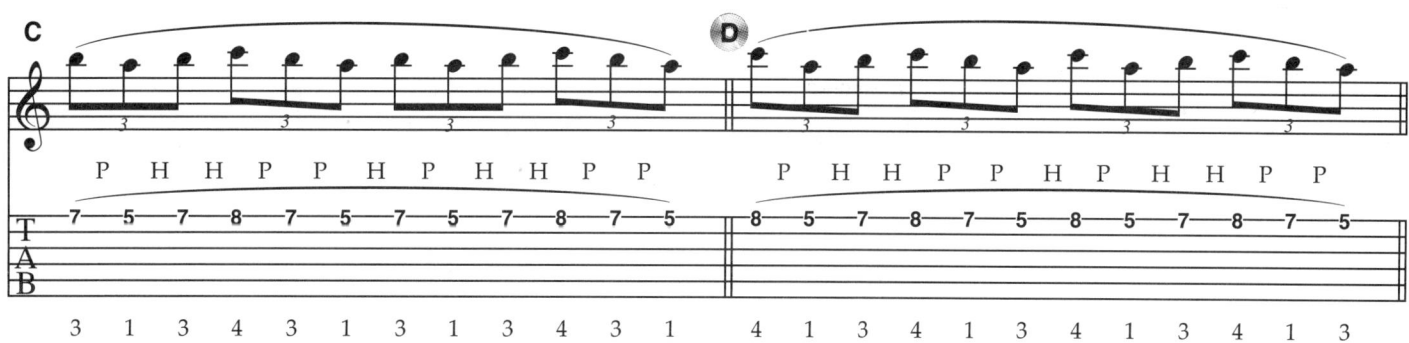

Here are some eighth-note ideas, but try them as sixteenth-note patterns as well.

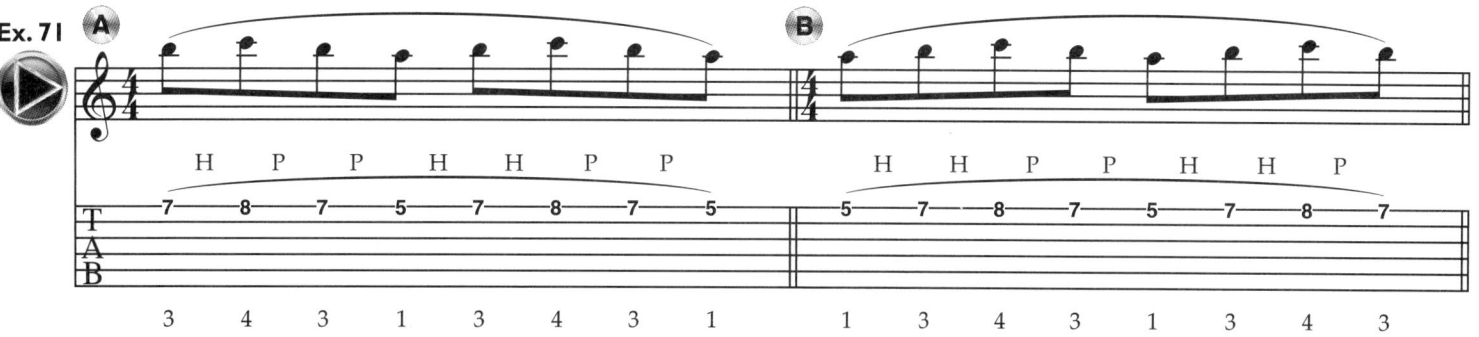

Shredding Guitar Workout

These patterns are more complex, as the rhythms are in five- or seven-note groupings.

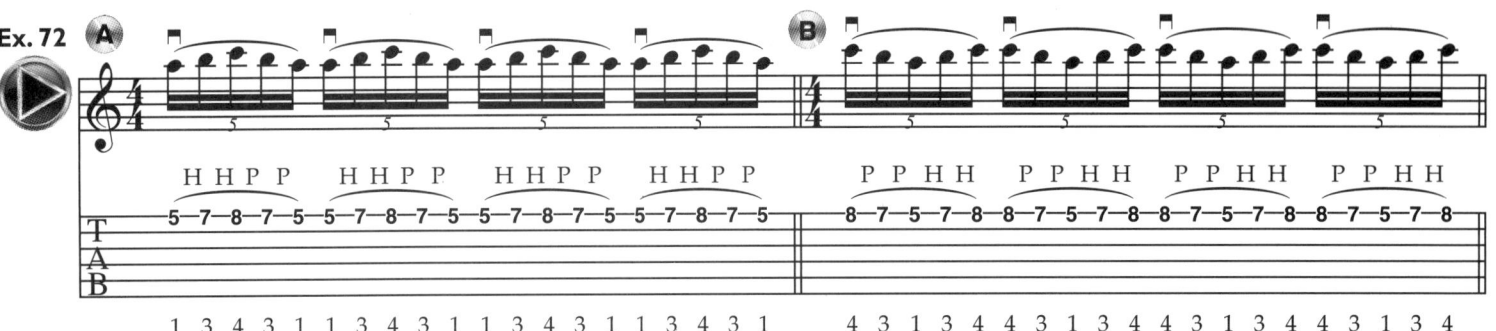

The following patterns will be a bit more challenging, as they involve two strings. Practice them slowly and make sure there is no unwanted noise when changing strings.

Ex. 73

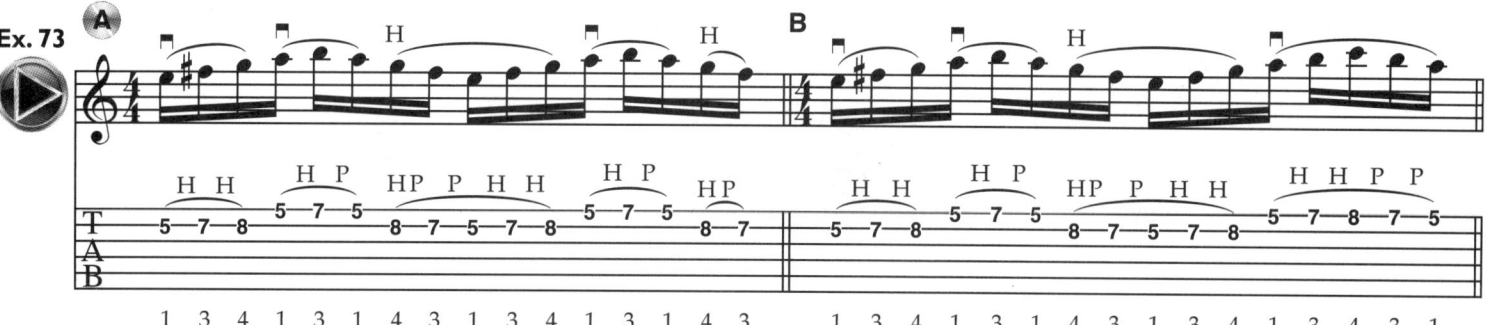
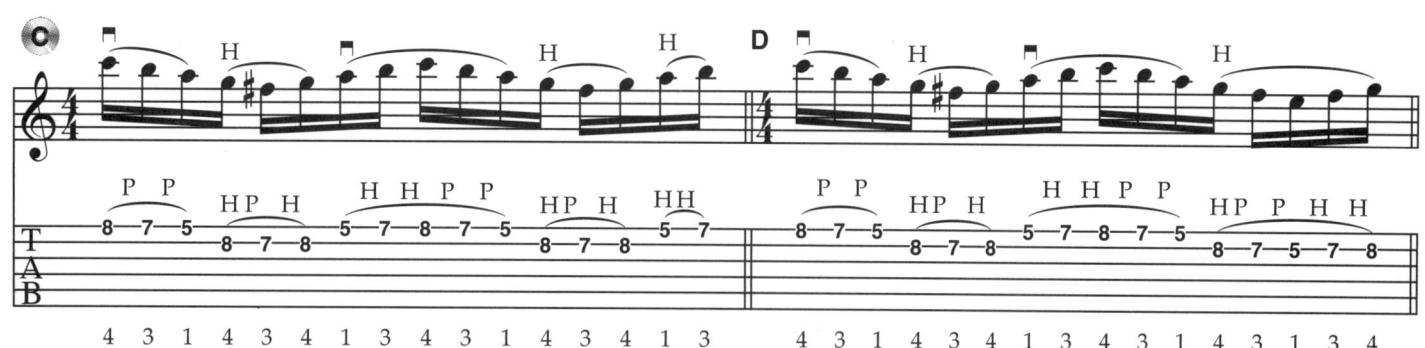
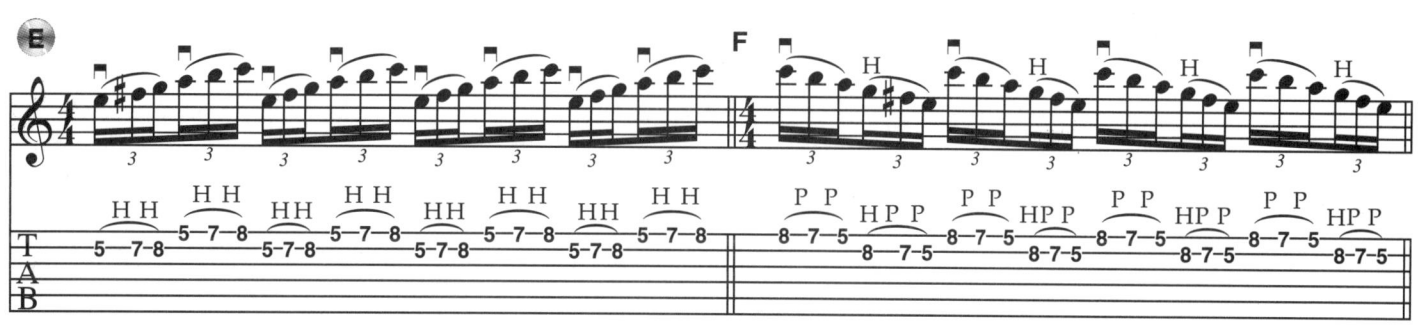

Shredding Guitar Workout

Legato Phrases Across the Fretboard

For the following ideas and patterns, we are using the three-note-per-string scales covered in the Alternate Picking chapter (see page 31). As always, use a metronome and don't forget to practice these examples in different keys.

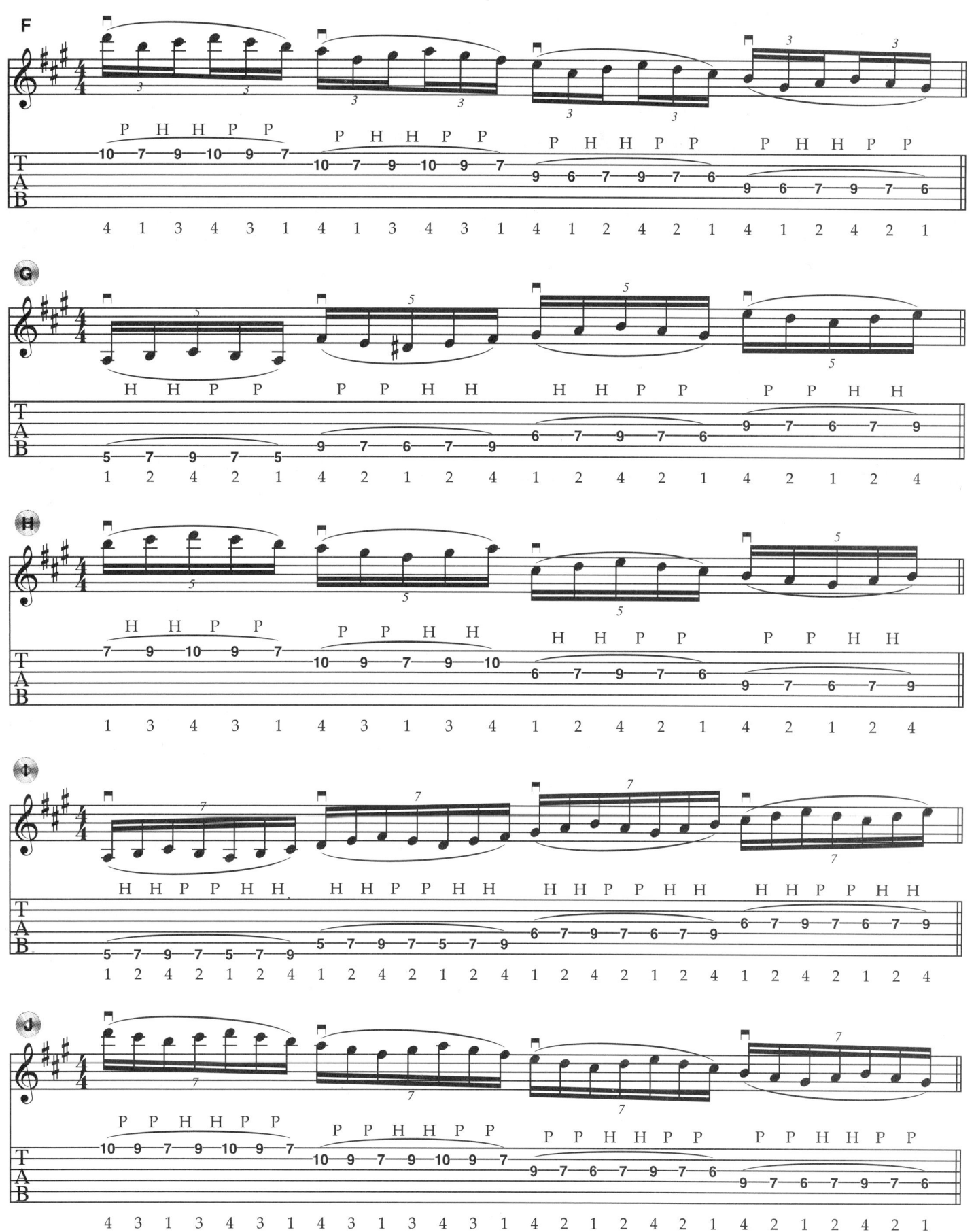

The next two examples illustrate a combination of the hexatonic patterns with an additional single-string pattern. Try to practice this ascending and descending idea using all available hexatonic patterns, covering three octaves.

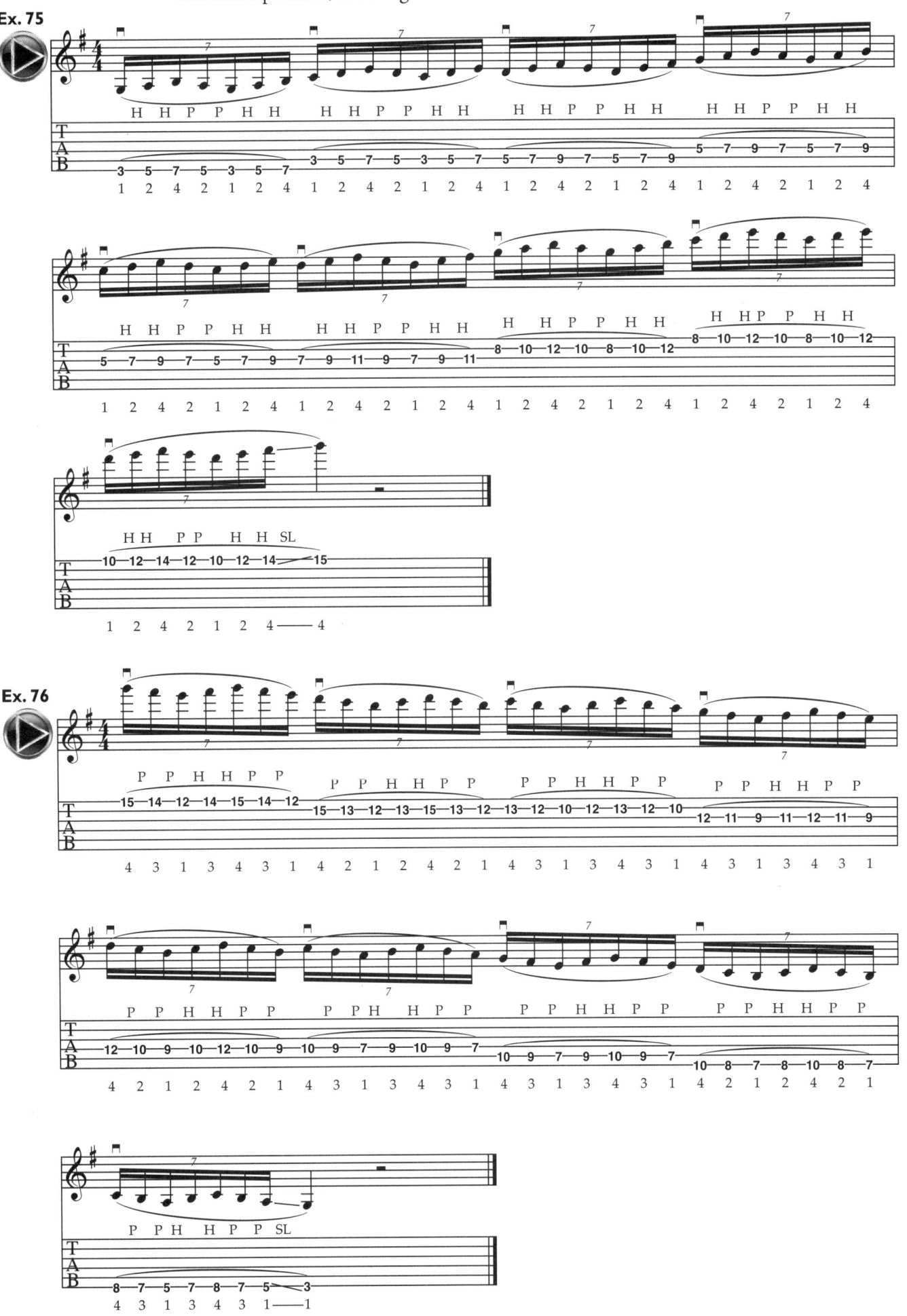

For an exciting sound, the lick below shows how to combine different legato patterns and string skipping.

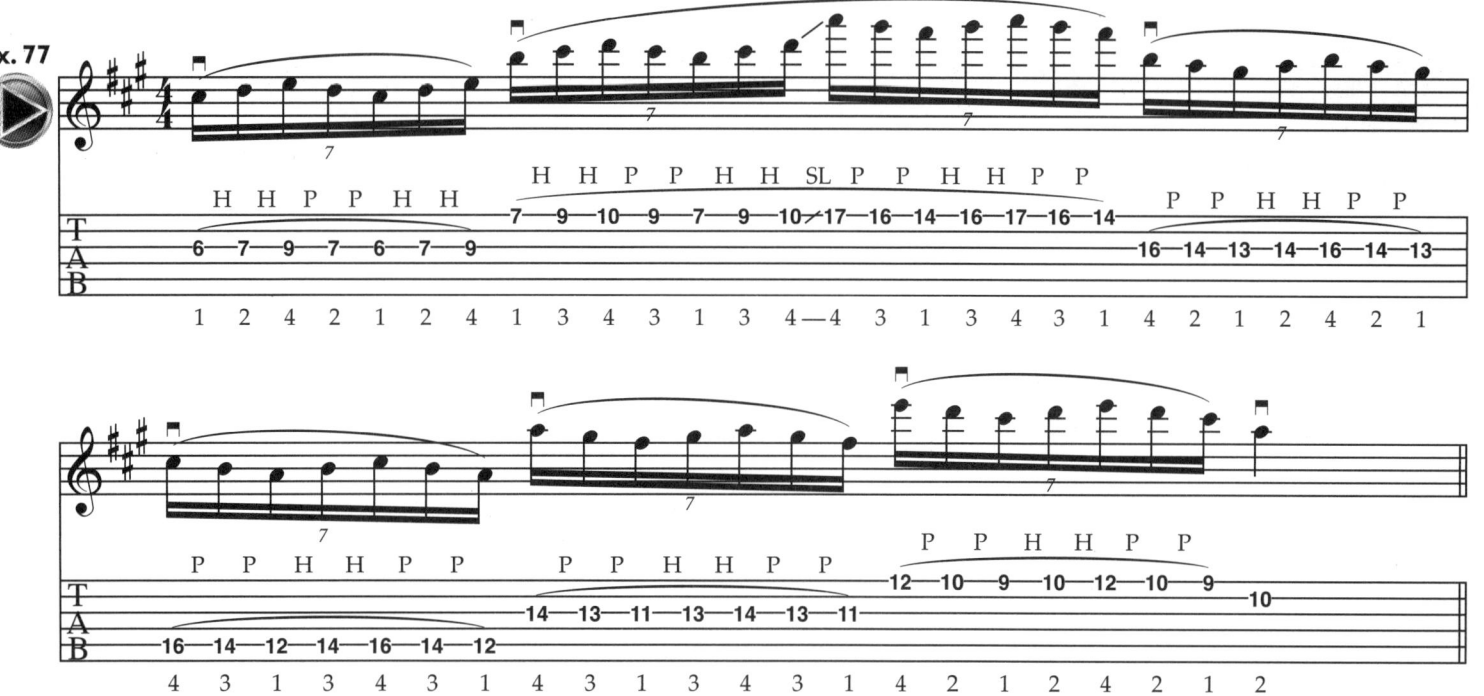

Ex. 77

The legato technique is a great way to create amazing-sounding lines and phrases. It requires a lot of practice and patience. Remember, make sure you are not using too much force to produce the notes when hammering-on or pulling-off, as this could affect the intonation and also sound very forced.

Precise placement of your fingers on the strings will ensure a great tone and will sound the string without using a lot of muscle.

Try to avoid using too much distortion, as it will not help your playing or sound. Rather, concentrate on getting a clear tone from your guitar and amp, and rely on excellent technique and ideas to produce great-sounding lines.

TAPPING

Tapping is a technique that utilizes the fingers of the picking hand to "tap" a note (or notes) against the fretboard at the appropriate fret. Tapping is often combined with legato techniques like hammer-ons and pull-offs to create a fluid, otherwordly sound.

Tapping requires great coordination between the left- and right-hand fingers. It is easiest to execute this technique when your tapping hand is stabilized by angling your thumb onto the fretboard.

T = Tap

There are a few basic tapping patterns at the core of this playing style, and they are demonstrated below using the A Minor Pentatonic scale.

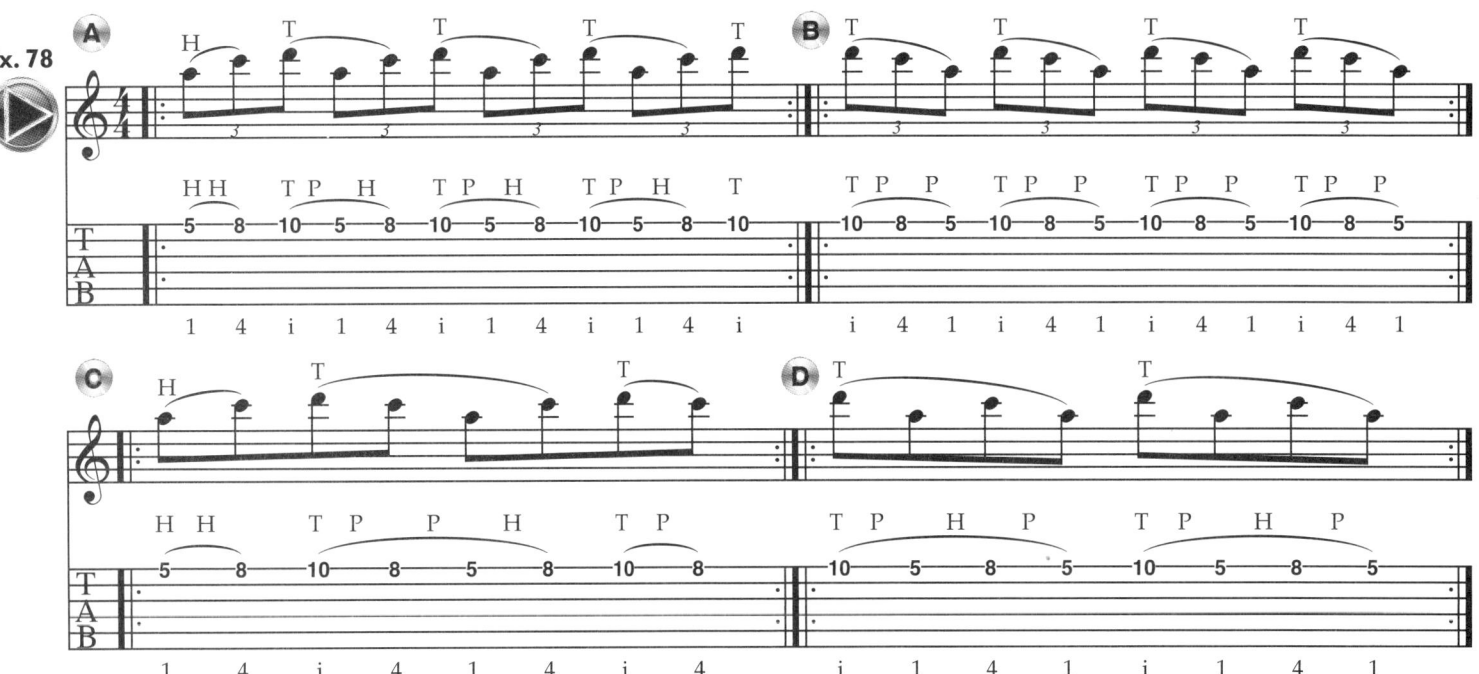

Apply the idea above to all pentatonic positions. In order to do that, combine all neighboring positions into *double pentatonics*. The diagram below combines two positions of the A Minor Pentatonic scale: one starting from the root and the other starting from the 3rd.

Tapping Adjacent Pentatonic Positions

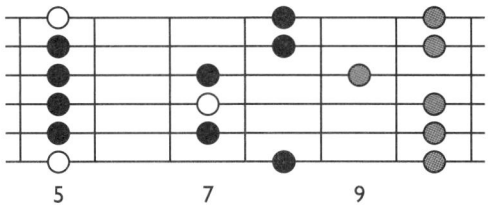

Combine the remaining positions and play these scales slowly up and down with tapping:

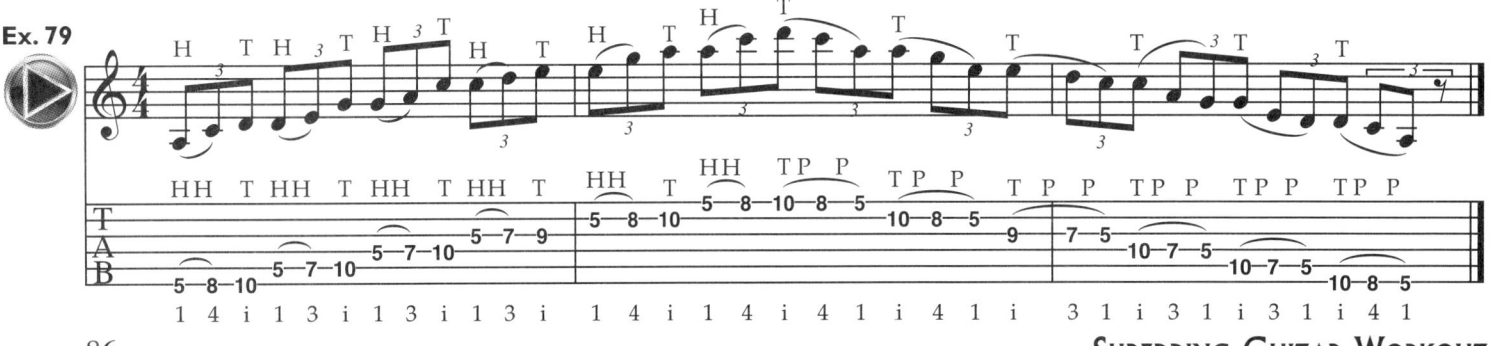

Shredding Guitar Workout

Another way to practice all possible positions is to play the pentatonic scale on adjacent string sets. Practice this idea on all possible strings and with the tapping patterns covered on the previous page.

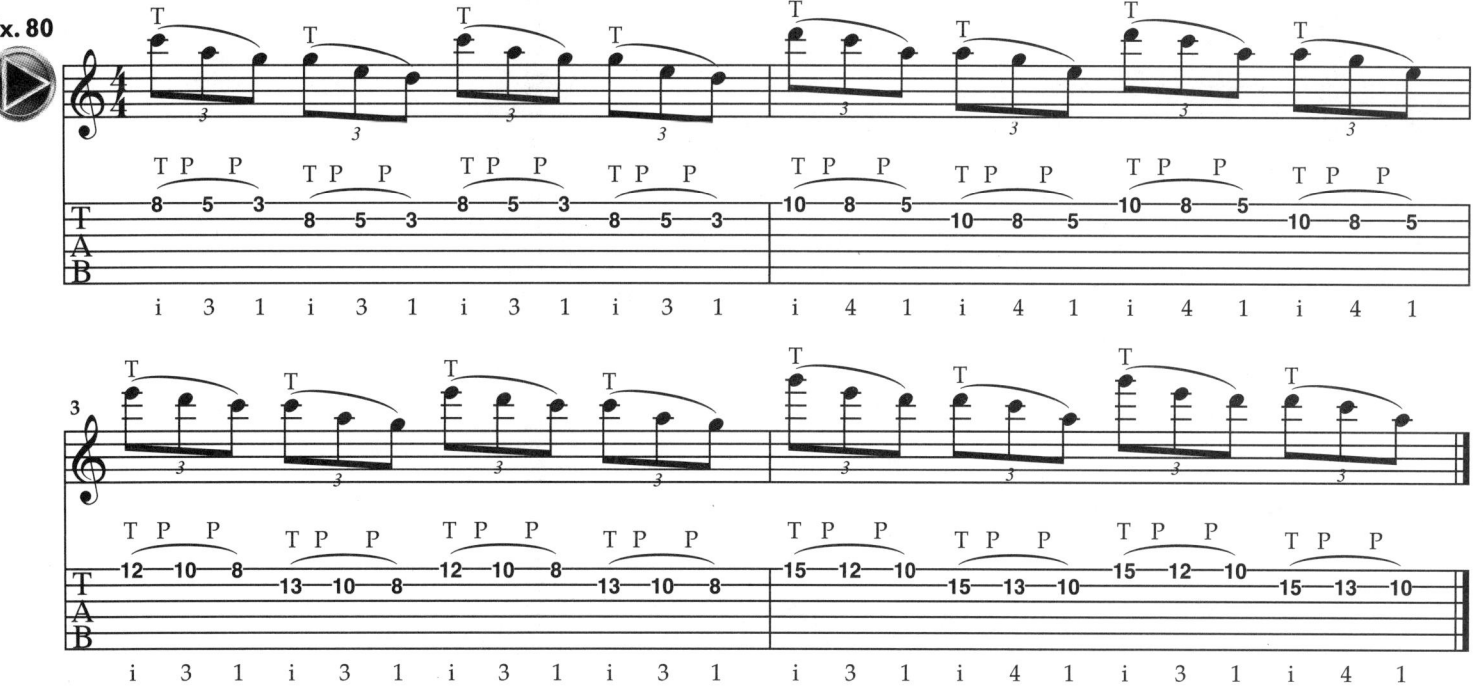

Ex. 80

Using the suggested basic patterns, practice the pentatonic combinations horizontally and vertically on the fretboard—and practice them in all 12 keys.

Another interesting way to organize the pentatonic scale is to use string skipping. The example below demonstrates the two basic shapes that can be derived from the previous double pentatonic shape.

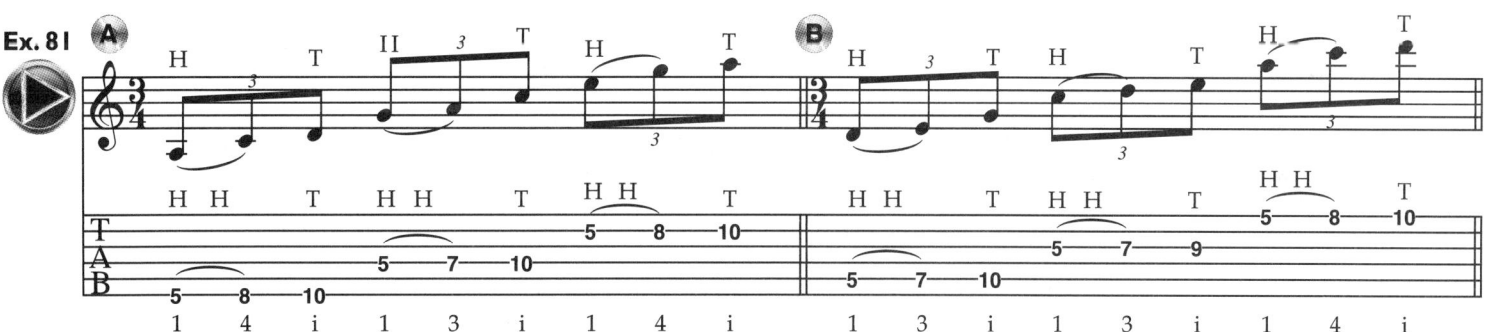

Ex. 81

Here is another variation on this idea, which takes the different shapes and creates a three-octave pentatonic scale encompassing several positions.

Ex. 82

Shredding Guitar Workout

The following example demonstrates a longer string-skipping idea utilizing a few different positions.

Ex. 83

Try to develop these different pentatonic tapping ideas into extended shapes. When practicing these lines, strive for an even tapping sound and don't fret or tap too hard, as the pitches of the notes can go sharp.

Here are some interesting ascending and descending pentatonic patterns. Try to develop some of your own as well!

Ex. 84
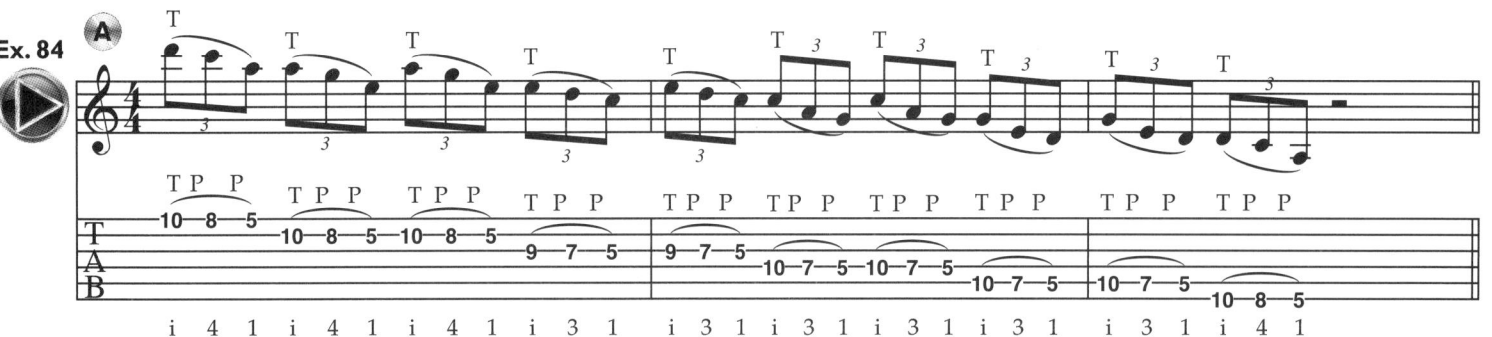

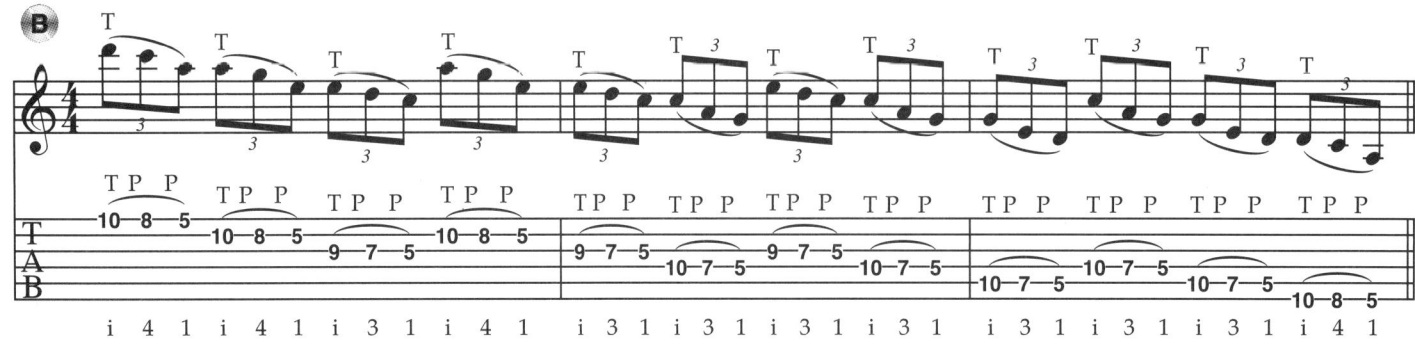

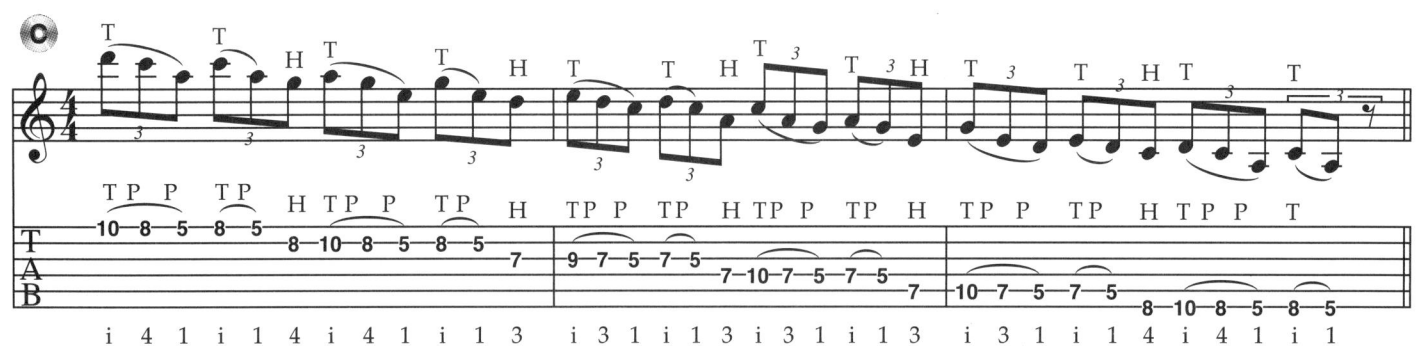

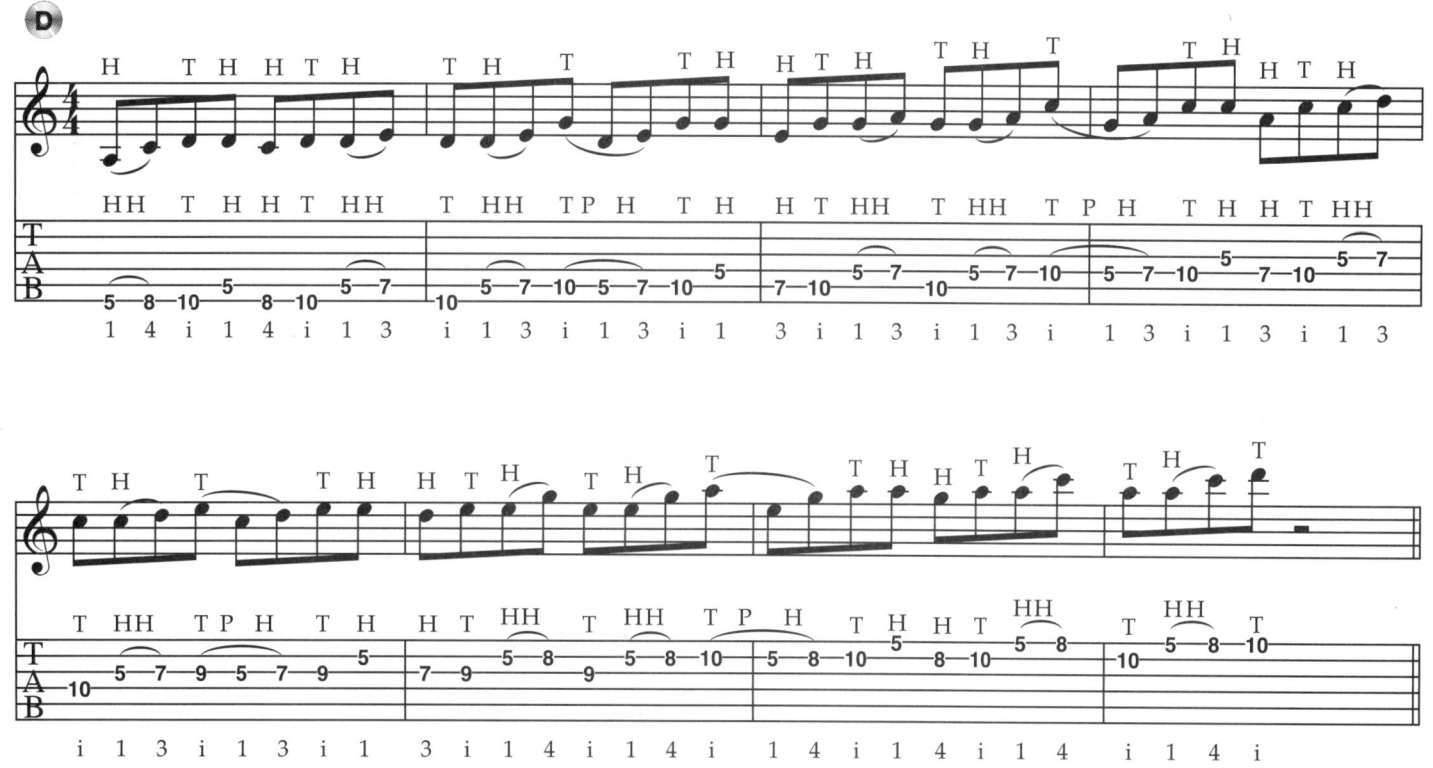

Tapping Scales and Arpeggios

Tapping has a very natural and fluid sound when applied to scales and arpeggios, opening up new ideas and possibilities. Tapping scales is relatively easy and involves one simple step: redistributing some notes to the tapping hand. The example below illustrates how a basic three-note-per-string scale is played using this approach. After mastering this concept, apply it to other scales as well.

Ex. 85

When practicing this technique, strive for an even sound, play accurately, and avoid too much pressure on the strings. Additionally, set your amp to a light overdrive without too much distortion.

The next examples are scale-based runs and phrases. Apply these ideas to different scales as well.

The next two examples utilize string skipping. Practice them as written, and then expand across the fretboard with other possible combinations of three- or four-note groupings per string.

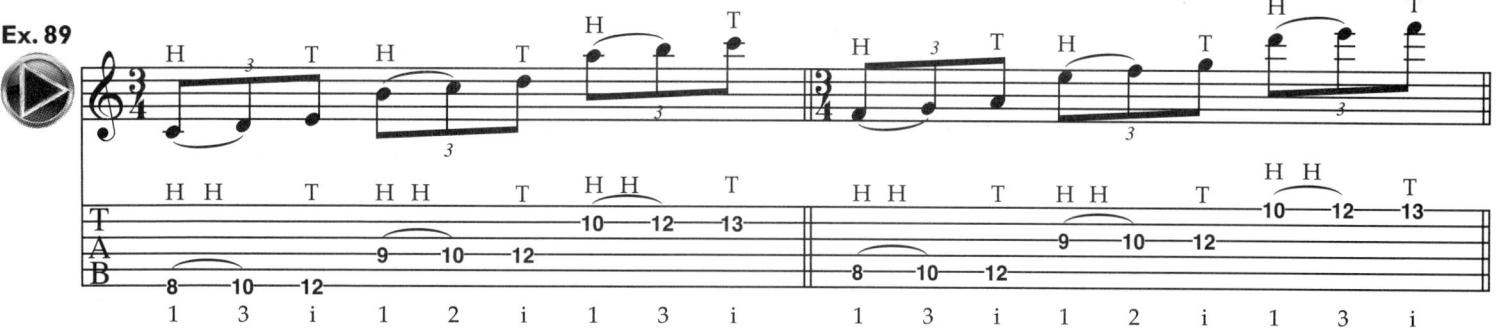

This example requires two fingers of your tapping hand, marked with *m* (middle finger) and *c* (pinky).

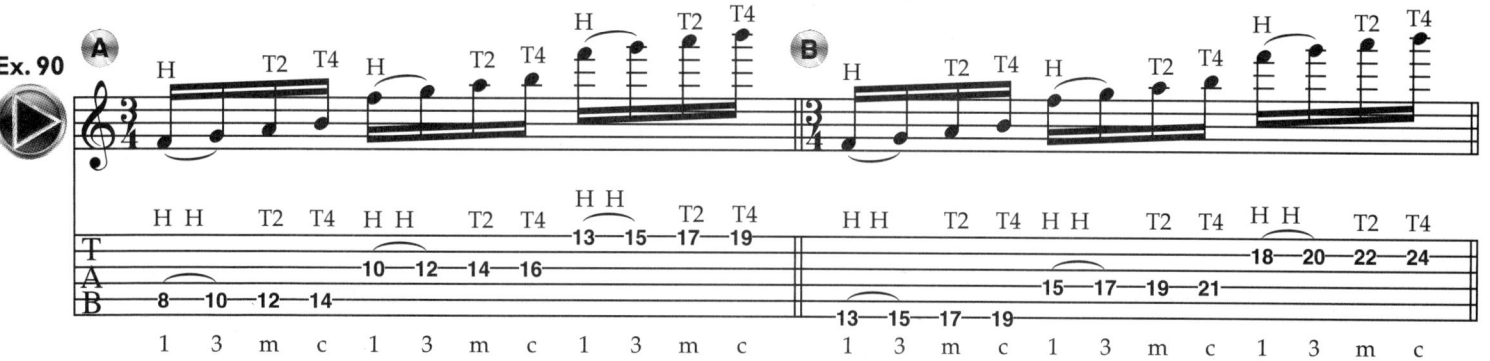

Of course, any of these scale-based shapes can be played in many different patterns. The following example shows a simple four-note ascending sequence.

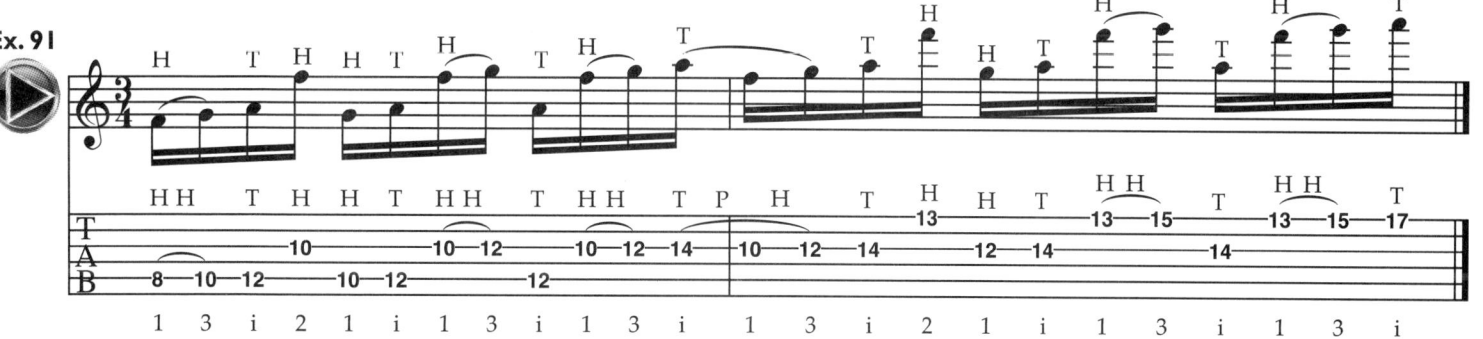

Try to combine these different scale excerpts and move them to different string sets, like E-D-B or A-G-E. There are a lot of interesting sounds to be discovered.

Tapping Triad Arpeggios

Now, let's extend what we've learned to playing triad arpeggios with tapping. The diagrams below include string skipping, and they show the root-position shapes for major, minor, diminished, and augmented arpeggios. These shapes can also be moved to the other set of three strings, or even extended by one or two strings when played on a seven- or eight-string guitar. Memorize these shapes, and play them ascending and descending in all 12 keys.

G Major

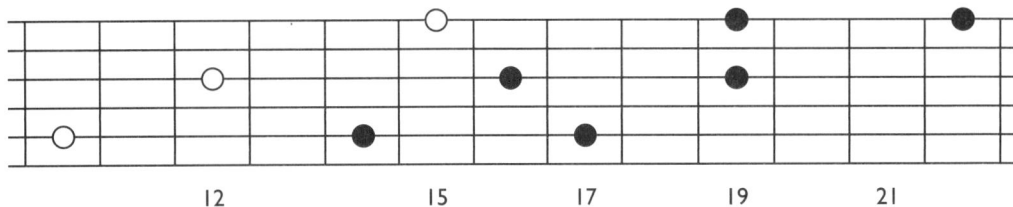

G Minor

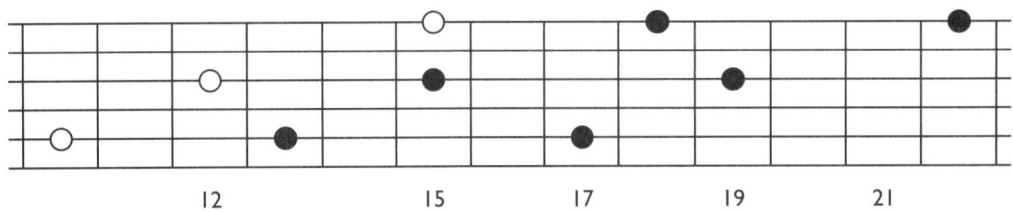

G Diminished

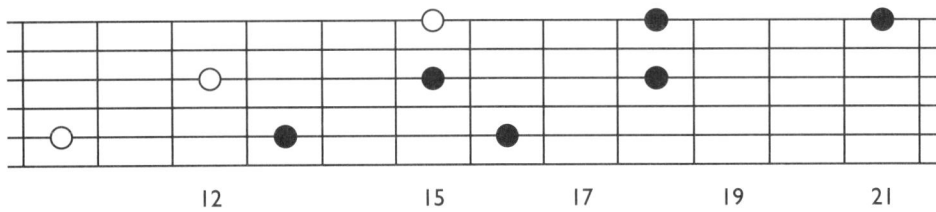

G Augmented

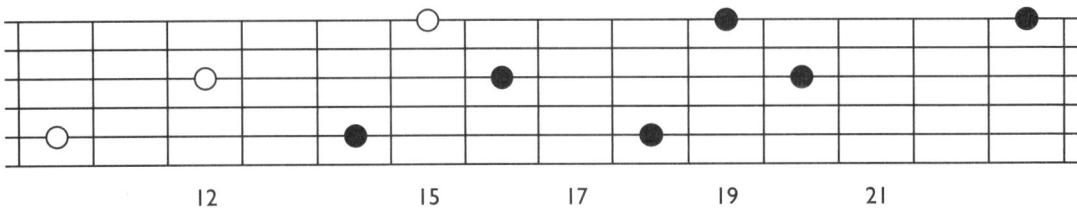

Here are some basic patterns for you to try. Remember, play them slowly and cleanly before attempting to play them faster.

Ex. 92

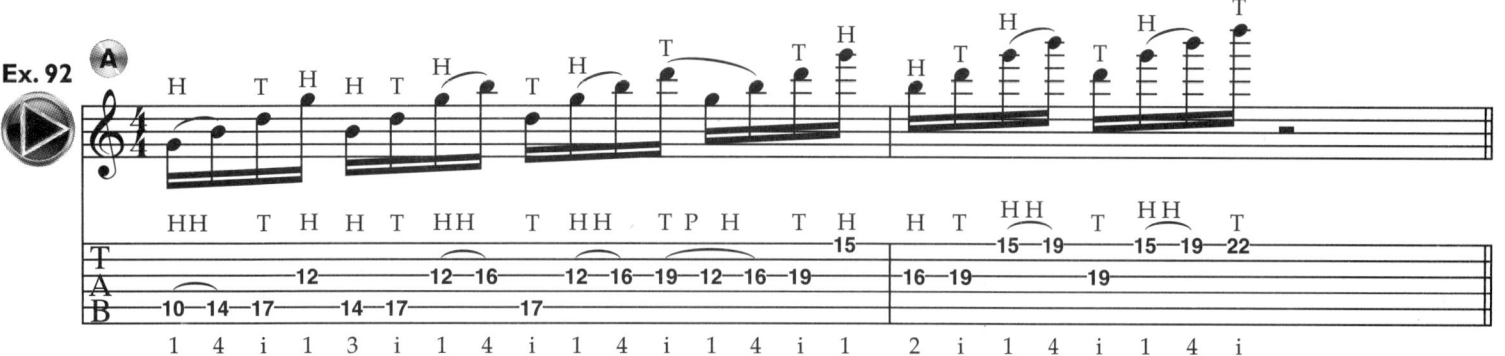

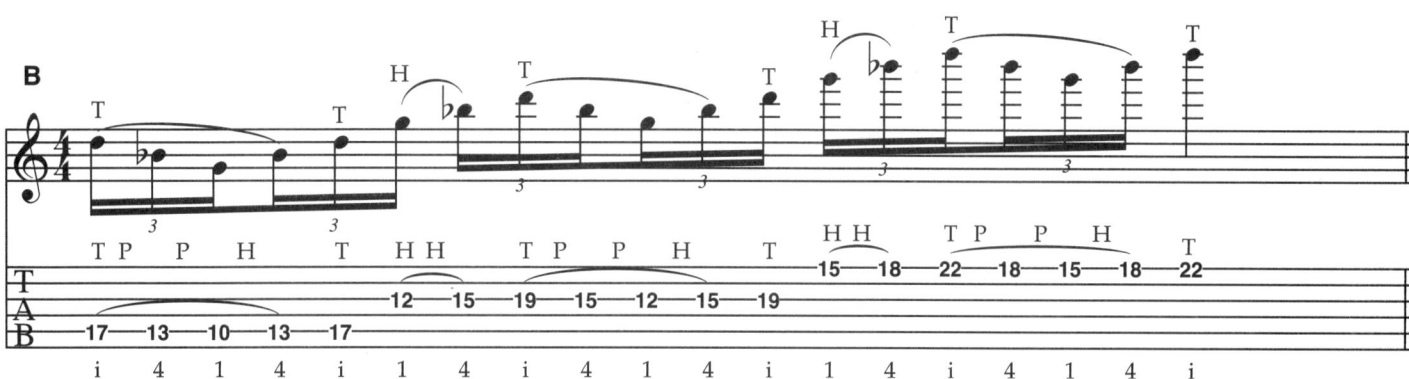

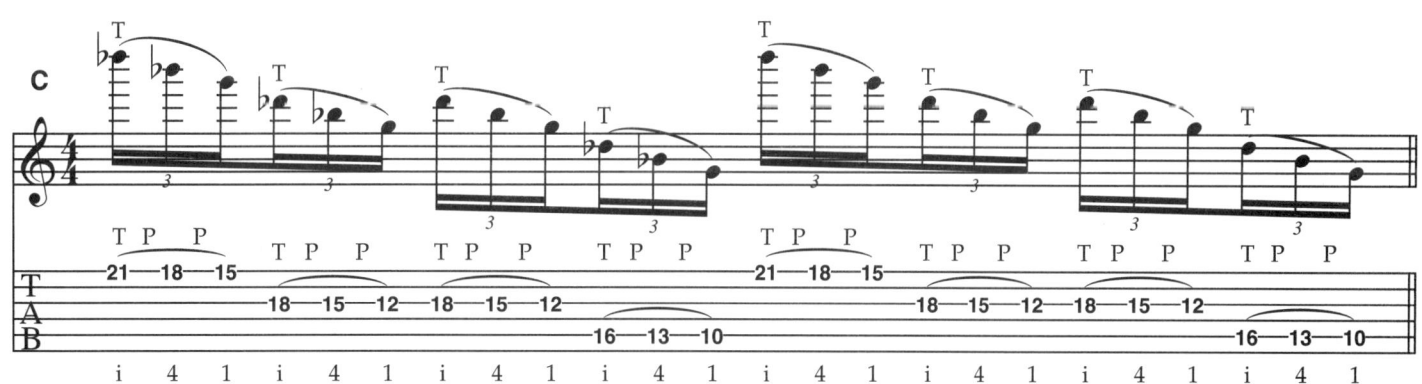

Try to find interesting songs from a songbook like *The Real Book* and arpeggiate the progressions, either straight up and down or with any of the patterns we've covered.

Tapping 7th Arpeggios

For more possibilities and extended sounds, let's take a look at playing 7th arpeggios with tapping. After you have learned and memorized the following shapes, try to harmonize all 12 major keys using this concept.

GMaj7

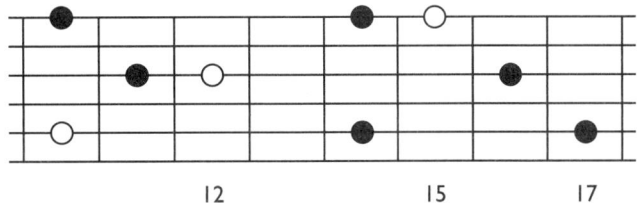

G7

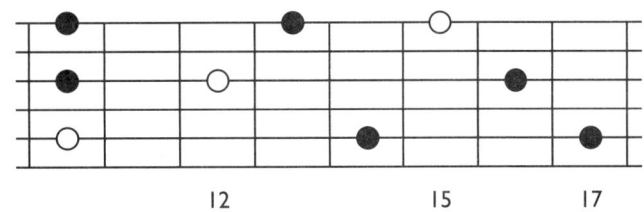

Gmin7

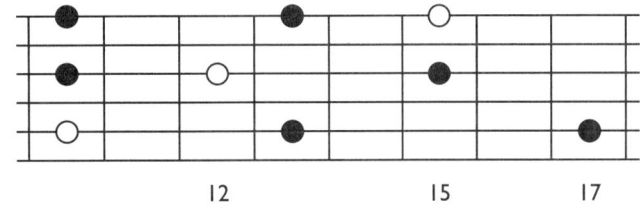

Gmin7♭5

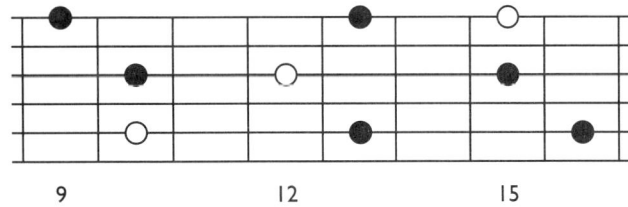

Gdim7

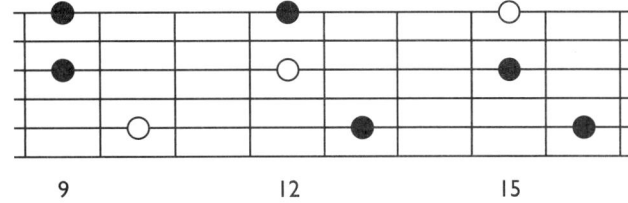

On the next page are some basic patterns and ideas. Play them slowly and evenly. Also, combine them in ascending and descending patterns, always striving for a smooth and fluid sound.

Try to come up with patterns of your own. Tapping arpeggios is a great way to develop different sounds and to explore interesting rhythmic ideas and phrasing.

SHREDDING GUITAR WORKOUT

CONCLUSION

Going forward, the goals and objectives to keep in mind are:
- Developing good alternate-picking technique
- Building scale and arpeggio sequence repertoire
- Increasing stamina and endurance
- Increasing speed and picking control
- Building sweep-picking arpeggio repertoire
- Developing legato technique
- Developing good intonation and fretting-hand strength
- Increasing fretboard and harmony knowledge by combining technique and theory exercises
- Developing tapping technique and building tapping repertoire

It's best to organize your material into categories and then pick and choose on a daily or weekly basis the desired content to be added to your practice regimen. In general, you should rotate the exercises within each of these categories, so that you are always practicing something new or different with the same objective. This way, you are adding to your skills and minimizing boring repetition.

Keeping a practice journal with a record of your goals, progress, and observations is critical to your success as a player. Reflecting upon your entries will help you stay motivated and will give you a clear, objective view of your achievements. It will also make it easier to identify your goals, as these tend to change when you grow as a musician.

Another important aspect to practicing is that it needs to be done in a musical context. Exercises will stay exercises if you don't apply them to your actual playing. It is important to apply what you learn to real musical situations in order to develop a fluent voice on the guitar, as well as your own style and repertoire.

Finally, my last advice for you is: Never give up! Never!